OTABIND®

Dear Friend:

You may have noticed that this book is put together differently than most other quality paperbacks. The page you are reading, for instance, along with the back page, is glued to the cover. And when you open the book the spine "floats" in back of the pages. But there's nothing wrong with your book. These features allow us to produce what is known as a detached cover, specifically designed to prevent the spine from cracking even after repeated use. A state-of-the-art binding technology known as OtaBind® is used in the manufacturing of this and all Health Communications, Inc. books.

HCI has invested in equipment and resources that ensure the books we produce are of the highest quality, yet remain affordable. At our Deerfield Beach headquarters, our editorial and art departments are just a few steps from our pressroom, bindery and shipping facilities. This internal production enables us to pay special attention to the needs of our readers when we create our books.

Our titles are written to help you improve the quality of your life. You may find yourself referring to this book repeatedly, and you may want to share it with family and friends who can also benefit from the information it contains. For these reasons, our books have to be durable and, more importantly, user-friendly.

OtaBind® gives us these qualities. Along with a crease-free spine, the book you have in your hands has some other characteristics you may not be aware of:

- Open the book to any page and it will lie flat, so you'll never have to worry about losing your place.
- You can bend the book over backwards without damage, allowing you to hold it with one hand.
- The spine is 3-5 times stronger than conventional perfect binding, preventing damage even with rough handling.

This all adds up to a better product for our readers—one that will last for years to come. We stand behind the quality of our books and guarantee that, if you're not completely satisfied, we'll replace the book or refund your money within 30 days of purchase. If you have any questions about this guarantee or our bookbinding process, please feel free to contact our customer service department at 1-800-851-9100.

We hope you enjoy the quality of this book, and find understanding, insight and direction for your life in the information it provides.

Peter Vegso
President

Health Communications, Inc.®
3201 S.W. 15th Street
Deerfield Beach, FL 33442-8190
(305) 360-0909

CONSUMING PASSIONS

Finding Real Love When Nothing Else Works

Robert F. Forman, Ph.D.

Health Communications, Inc.
Deerfield Beach, Florida

Library of Congress Cataloging–in–Publication Data

Forman, Robert F.
Consuming passions: finding real love when nothing else works/Robert F. Forman.
p. cm.
ISBN 1-55874-303-0
1. Compulsive behavior 2. Love. I. Title.
RC533.F67 1994
94-15461
158.1—dc20 CIP

ISBN 1-55874-298-0

Publisher: Health Communications, Inc.
3201 S.W. 15th Street
Deerfield Beach, Florida 33442-8190

Cover design by Robert Cannata

To my grandmother Irene

Romantic love is mental illness. But it's a pleasurable one. It's a drug. It distorts reality, and that's the point of it.

—Fran Lebowitz

ACKNOWLEDGMENTS & ACCUSATIONS

I hardly ever read the acknowledgement section of books because they are usually boring thanks to people I don't know. Since the editor has repeatedly asked me to write one, I'll do my best to not waste the paper. But who really should be acknowledged?

Should I mention those second grade classmates who stole my hat and tossed it amongst themselves while I tried vainly to retrieve it? Monkey in the middle. Somehow, today, I think of them. Or how about Michele—I think that was her name. At the skating rink I slipped and fell for her so hard. Icily she scorned my awkward teenage overtures; I couldn't eat for days afterward. Shards of my first broken heart still rattle around in me. There are others worth mentioning, but I'll spare you.

There's a room full of ghosts who deserve credit, too. Dope-buddies who overdosed and went to the other side; others who've lived on—psychotic and scrambled. These were the people with whom I lived under the influence. In our consensual fog, we huddled together over bongs, bottles and lines doing the best we could.

I am grateful to all of these people who have contributed, quite innocently, to the pain which served as the catalyst for this book. Fortunately, they are not the only ones who deserve recognition.

Like the air I breathe, I've never known a day without my family's love. My mother, my father, my brother and my sister. Through thick and thicker, I could always count on them. And thanks for always asking "how's the book doing?"

Next I think about my cats. One is on the computer monitor right now; another is warming herself by sitting in the well of my printer. Why acknowledge these fur balls? Because they seem to love me the most when I have felt the most alone. The last chapter was co-authored by them.

There are thousands of members of 12-Step Fellowships from whom I've stolen much of what's in this book. All my years studying psychology didn't teach me what you have. It's through you that I hear the whispers of God.

Finally, having made my more flowery acknowledgements, I want to thank all the nuts-and-bolt folk who *really* made this book possible. Thank you Yvonne Kaye, for pushing me to write and giving me the number for Health Communications. You passed it on to me. Thank you Mark Shogal, for being my tireless writing coach, conscience and collaborator. Thanks for all those Sunday afternoons. Special thanks to Barbara Nichols for reading my book proposal, signing me up and nudging me ever so gently along. Good luck to you on your continuing journey. Also, special thanks to Jay Efran, Rob Wozniak, Hal Sands and Clark McCauley for finding room for me under your professorial wings. Thanks to Jeff and Elizabeth at the Sweet Potato Café for letting me move into one of their booths while writing and re-writing this book. Ditto to Borders Bookstore/Café. And finally, to Christine Belleris and Homer Pyle for tucking this book in and helping to get it to press.

Oh yes—a final, final acknowledgment. There are friends and colleagues who'd be really peeved if I didn't mention them in this acknowledgment section: Karen Cutler, Fred Mulligan, Tom Gibbons, Paddi Ann McGinnis and Charlotte Malvestuto Royer—they keep Rehab After Work working; Ann Cariola for doing the same at Haverford.

Contents

Introduction xi

Part One: The Lovesickness Disease

1. The Lovesickness Process 3
2. Sources Of Lovesickness 21
3. Lovesickness And The Addictions 43

Part Two: The Lovesickness Cure

4. Reliable Sources Of Unconditional Love 69
5. God As A Reliable Source Of Unconditional Love . . . 81
6. Talking To Ourselves 105
7. Treating Yourself With Unconditional Love 121
8. Find A Loving Community 141
9. Take Two Puppies And Call Me In The Morning . . . 157

Resources 165
Support & Recovery Groups 169
Love Quotes 182

INTRODUCTION

About 11 years ago it hit me. I did not figure it out. I did not apply logic, scholarship or even hard work, at least not in the usual sense. Quite simply, I was minding my own business, going about my embarrassing and intoxicated life the best I could. Then the revelations began.

The first veil lifted when a girlfriend dumped me. The details are somewhat blurred, but this much I recall: Things were not going especially well with the relationship. I was broke, unfaithful and having a tough time coping with graduate school and earning my daily stale bread. When the time came for this girlfriend *du jour* to gather up her self-esteem and tell me to kiss off, I was too numb to care.

Later, however, I noticed I was alone.

It was a Sunday morning. I'd awakened to a trashy apartment with old bills and clothes scattered about. For companionship, I turned on the television. On that morning, PBS was running a tape of Leo Buscaglia. Leo was sweating and ranting and waving his hands while talking about love.

I don't exactly know what Leo said on that morning, but I do remember coming to the following conclusions: I did not love myself, I had not loved my most recent ex-girlfriend or perhaps any of my past girlfriends and in general I was a pretty screwed up guy. This was an astounding turnaround for me; up until that moment I thought I was doing just fine.

Ashamed—For A Moment

That morning I was disgusted with myself and ashamed of what I had become. At once I was committed to becoming a more loving and complete human being.

Satisfied and impressed with my new found self-awareness, I filled a bowl of pot, got high and drifted off to the land of Oz.

Not surprisingly, nothing changed about me or my relationships in the months to come. I wanted to change but hadn't yet figured out what or how to do it. For the first time, however, I understood that something was wrong.

For several more months my social and romantic life continued to weave a loose fabric of drugs, superficial intimacies and nausea. Meanwhile, my professional life was taking me across some curious terrain.

For six or seven years I had been working as an addictions counselor. I worked in a prison with alcohol- and drug-addicted inmates. I worked as an interviewer for a county drunk driving program. I worked at a weight loss center. And I worked as a professor of addiction studies at a small liberal arts college. Through it all, I religiously got high. It's impressive how effectively Visine gets the red out.

In bars I would encounter people I had sent off to treatment. In dope dealers' apartments I would encounter past patients. In my dreams the police would track me down and arrest me.

At these various jobs, my clients and employers expected me to know a little something about addiction. Sadly, I'd learned nothing about the subject in school. To make up for my deficiencies, I began attending open lectures and open meetings of Alcoholics Anonymous. At these A.A. meetings I found myself identifying with parts of the stories I heard. At lectures on addiction, I'd sink down uncomfortably into my chair, feeling exposed. Occasionally I'd think that maybe, just maybe I was an addict. Then I would reconsider. I stopped attending lectures.

Around 1980 the *Diagnostic and Statistical Manual III-Revised (DSMIII-R)* was released by the American Psychiatric Association. The *DSMIII-R* is the official book of psychiatric diagnoses, and this new edition offered a greatly improved description of addiction. Given my professional responsibilities as well as my personal irresponsibilities, I was anxious to see what the new diagnostic manual had to say.

As luck would have it, I was right there in the manual, in black and white. Not only was my substance use neatly described—so was my "love" life. My relationships with women bore a striking resemblance to my relationship with mood-altering chemicals.

Tolerance For Women

Loss of control. Attempts at control. Adverse consequences. Preoccupation. These were some of the symptoms of addiction. I could even see that I had developed a type of tolerance for every woman I had ever become involved with. Initially, upon falling in love, I'd be in ecstasy. Yet, invariably, with increasing intimacies and repetition, the euphoria that I'd felt at first would diminish and then disappear. Finally, whenever I or the woman would bring our relationship to a halt, I would experience an intense withdrawal syndrome (which I'd promptly medicate with my favorite non-nutritional supplements).

Initially, I didn't know if I was the only one who had these experiences or if everyone did. I also didn't know if other addiction professionals were aware of this phenomena. I hadn't read anything about it, but then again I wasn't the greatest scholar in the world either.

After the "aha" of my discovery wore off, I tucked this curiosity away in a dusty corner of my mind for later consideration. I had other distractions to attend to; there was no time for disturbing thoughts.

Despite my sincerest intentions to remain in denial, bits and pieces of the addiction puzzle began showing up in front of me.

One day I came across Stanton Peele's book entitled *Love And Addiction* (Peele and Brodsky 1975). Peele had recognized that love could look like addiction or be an addictive process. Peele said that relationships could be viewed as loving or addictive depending upon whether the relationship enhanced the well-being of the partners or if it hurt them. Although Peele's focus was on love, not addictions, as far as I know he was one of the first to make the love/addiction connection.

About the same time that I came across *Love And Addiction*, I wandered into the office of Dr. Howard Hoffman. Dr. Hoffman was a professor of psychology at Bryn Mawr College, where I was doing my graduate work. In lieu of working on my dissertation, I often wandered the halls looking for someone to distract me. On this particular occasion, I struck up a conversation with Dr. Hoffman about his work in the area of attachment and how mothers and their babies develop their emotional bonds. In the course of this discussion, Dr. Hoffman told me about the work of researcher Jaak Panksepp of Bowling Green State University in Ohio.

Panksepp, it turned out, found he could manipulate the mother/infant attachment process in animals by fooling around with the animal's endorphin system (the body's natural opiate supplier). For example, if he gave a baby guinea pig an endorphin-like substance such as morphine, the guinea pig would ignore its mother and fail to bond with her. If he gave it Naloxone, a drug that blocked the endorphin system, guinea pigs would act as if their mother had been taken away—even if the mother was right there with them. The baby guinea pigs would squeal and cry.

On the other hand, if baby guinea pigs were given morphine and then removed from their mothers, their normal separation distress would be eliminated. They did not cry for their mother. Panksepp found that a similar disruption in the mother/infant bonding could be created by manipulating the mother's endorphin system, too. Thus, either partner in the mother/infant relationship could be turned indifferent with a small dose of morphine. It is important to point out that other sedating drugs, such as barbiturates and tranquilizers, do not have this effect on mother/infant bonding. Somehow the endorphin system was involved in at least one form of "love."

Panksepp concluded by suggesting that the attachment that develops between mothers and their babies was mediated by activity in the endorphin system. In addition, he suggested that perhaps all social attachments, including those that take place later in life, may be dependent upon the healthy functioning of the endorphin system. He and others have noted that alcoholics and other addicts were notorious for having poor romantic and social relations. They also generally had a disturbance in their endorphin system. Hmmm.

A Biochemical Clue

Panksepp's work unleashed a swirl of new questions in my mind. I now had a biochemical clue that linked addiction and love relations (or bonding). I didn't understand how this tidbit of information fit into my emerging understanding of myself or of the way addiction works, but I knew it did fit. If only I could find out how.

With this new information, I began to look at the patients I was working with through new eyes. At the prison where I worked, I noticed that all the inmates in my therapy group had several things in common. First, one or both of their parents were either alcohol- or drug-addicted (thus creating the likelihood that the mother/infant bonding had been impaired). Second, as the inmates described their addiction, and especially their relapse history, the same theme appeared in case after case.

The typical story went something like this: John was arrested for burglary and it was determined that he would benefit from a stay in prison. While there, John attended A.A. meetings and was given addiction counseling.

Upon completing his sentence, John was released with recommendations to continue in counseling and attend meetings of A.A. or Narcotics Anonymous. Unfortunately, before too long, usually within six months to a year, John would be back in prison and back in my therapy group.

Love As An Antidote

When asked what happened, John would describe how he

had been going to A.A. meetings and staying sober. He'd gotten a job and was doing okay. Then he met a girl and fell in love. Being in love made him feel so wonderful that his desire to drink was completely removed. Not only that, he felt the strength and courage to forge out into the world and find an extra job so he could make more money. Naturally, he cut back on his A.A. meetings and therapy—hell, he felt so good that he was sure he had no need for such things anymore. After a week, a month or maybe several months of romantic bliss, the ground would disappear from beneath him. It would start with a fight, then a breakup and end in relapse. He was back on the booze or back on the drugs, and soon he was back on the sheriff's bus heading once again for the "Grey Bar Hotel."

The craving for addictive substances was removed when my clients fell in love. Their new love became their drug substitute. It filled their opiate receptors in the same way that alcohol or heroin did. But eventually the euphoria would vanish. Upon careful questioning they would usually acknowledge having become disinterested, neglectful or even unfaithful to their girlfriends. A fight would soon follow and then a rapid return to substance use.

Again and again I'd hear variations of this same tale. During my first couple of years counseling in the prison, I thought it was just one of the array of jailhouse cons ("Hey, man. Cut me a break. My ol' lady dumped me . . ."). Now, however, I was seeing more pieces to the puzzle.

In fact, I was now finding new connections everywhere I looked. I came across research by Simpson, O'Brian and Whitfield in which they independently reported that withdrawal symptoms in alcoholics (e.g., delirium tremens, convulsions, hallucinations) could be dramatically reduced with a little tender loving attention from their nurses and counselors. Interaction with caring counselors helped to reduce or prevent serious withdrawal symptoms in late stage alcoholics. Somehow, love and attention had the power of strong medication even in physically dependent alcoholics.

Meanwhile, while working in a local high school with chemically dependent teenagers, I noticed that instead of writing the names of a boyfriend or girlfriend on their notebooks, jeans and sneakers, my chemically dependent teens wrote the names of their favorite brand of beer or drew pictures of marijuana leaves. Were these inscriptions declarations of love and commitment? Rather than mooning over "Darla" or "Dave," were these young people in love with a drug?

Drugs And Love Interchangeable

And then, of course, there was me.

I noticed that I experienced the same gnawing feeling in my gut regardless of whether I was waiting for my girlfriend to show up or waiting to buy some drugs. More and more, the distinctions began to blend. I could see that for me drugs and women were completely interchangeable. Only drugs and alcohol were easier to come by.

Amidst all these revelations, my addictions continued in full force. Insight alone was not translating into action. At least not yet.

Then along came the Spring of 1983. Spring is the best time to be in love and the worst time to be alone. I was alone. I dreaded going through the spring without a girlfriend. What could I do? I could no longer call my old girlfriends; that was getting humiliating. I had to find someone new and in a hurry.

One day, as I was leaving the prison, I saw an inmate being released. Waiting for him was a luscious young woman who was obviously his girlfriend. She embraced him passionately as soon as he was freed. Seeing this, my depression turned three shades darker.

The fact that I was girlfriendless was bad enough. That an inmate—a convicted felon—was walking into the arms of a beautiful woman was absolutely unbearable.

As usual, I pulled my buddy, the pipe, out from under the car seat. "No brain, no pain." Although I was bored with getting high, I didn't have anything else in my repertoire to deal with feeling unloved.

And then I got an idea. "That's okay, Bob," I said to myself. "I love you, anyway." It struck me as a peculiar thing to say, but also reasonable. I began to repeat to myself: "I love you, Bob. I love you, Bob. I love you, Bob." I must have said it two dozen times. It made me laugh out loud.

Suddenly, it was obvious to me: my real problem was that I needed love. How simple. But not love from one single individual. That didn't seem to work too well. I needed to find some nonchemical, nonromantic ways to fill the void — to fill the emptiness and inadequacy that had dominated my life. I needed to find a love I could count on.

This book describes what I found. Today I know that I am not the only one with this need; indeed, I tend to think most people have it.

In the ten years since I first hit upon these ideas, I have continued to work with addicted individuals of all kinds: compulsive overeaters, co-dependents, compulsive spenders, gamblers, sex and love addicts and hundreds of alcoholics and drug addicts. The information that follows is about all of them—and about me and you.

What Is Lovesickness?

In the first chapter of this book, I dissect the underlying dynamics of lovesickness and addiction. I use the term "lovesickness" to describe the internal, subjective experience that drives addictive behavior. I describe those symptoms that cut across all categories of addictive behavior. And I make the case that lovesickness applies to a wide range of other troublesome behaviors that normally are not viewed as addictions.

The second chapter describes the possible causes of lovesickness. Here I attempt to reconcile the available genetic and biochemical research with the more psychosocial theories of addiction.

In the third chapter, the many possible manifestations of lovesickness are described: greed, the shop-till-you-drop impulse, work addiction, compulsive sex. Readers should not be surprised if they find themselves more than once in these paragraphs. The net is thrown widely so that many destructive behavior patterns can be viewed from within the lovesick framework.

Having described lovesickness, its causes and manifestations, we then move on to map out strategies for recovery. Within the context of the Lovesickness Theory, it becomes possible to understand why some people successfully change and others do not. It also helps us to find a rationale for some of the peculiar paths that recovering people have taken over the years.

In the subsequent five chapters, I describe specific sources of real love that can be counted upon. This is the good stuff—genuine soul food. There are three and a half reliable sources of unconditional love. Each is described in detail, providing practical techniques for accessing all of them.

Ten years ago, when I first attempted to write about what I was learning, I realized that lovesickness was the most appropriate term I could use. On the one hand, the emotions I was trying to understand felt like love. But why was it all so sick? Today I understand that, like so many other people, I was looking for love in all the wrong places.

Lovesickness offers an explanation and a way out of our addictive and destructive relationships with people and things. By applying the strategies for recovery and personal growth presented here, people should be able to free themselves and move on to a fuller, healthier life—a life full of love and freedom.

PART ONE

The Lovesickness Disease

CHAPTER 1

The Lovesickness Process

Our soul needs love as much as our body needs food and water. After our physical requirements for nourishment and safety have been met, the search for love begins. We all need love and we will do very strange things if we do not get enough of it.

Most people are terribly confused about love. On the one hand, everywhere we turn, love stories abound. Songs, movies, television—even greeting cards—speak of love. Year after year, books about love ascend the best-sellers charts while gothic and modern romance novels faithfully break sales records. With so much talking, writing, reading and singing about love, why is there such a shortage of the stuff?

The answer is found as we unravel the tangle of Cupid's many lustrous curls. There is no shortage of love; in fact there truly is an infinite supply. The problem is that we choose love poorly. Finding our way out of the web of "lovelack" depends solely on making better choices. The ability to choose well in love is perhaps the greatest challenge facing each of us as individuals and as a species. More than anything, this book is about the kinds of things we "fall in love with" versus the kinds of love we can choose.

Ooooh Baby, Baby-itis

Almost everyone has had the experience of falling in love. For most people the first encounter came sometime during the spring of adolescence. Others may have called it "puppy love" or a "crush," but when it was happening to us it was the most important event of our lives. Adults observing teenagers going through this collision with infatuation tend to discount it as being not much more than some kind of hormonal uprising—it's cute when the relationship remains innocent, a nuisance when there's only one telephone in the house and a crisis when parents discover that their teen's libidinal urges have been consummated.

Adolescent Love Sets The Stage

Falling in love may actually be one of life's most important phenomena. Indeed, these early experiences of adolescent love appear to serve as a primary organizing pattern for the rest of our lives. It's not just that these early love affairs provide the template for evaluating our future love relations—although this in itself is certainly important. Of even greater significance is the fact that how we work, how we play, what we dread and, most especially, what we yearn for are first revealed during these early encounters of the romantic kind.

I'd like you to pause for a minute and think about a time when you fell head-over-heels, palms sweating, heart-pounding, crazy in love. You know, the time when the world stood still and the sun shone through the night. No, this isn't about mature, growing-together love, nor is it about love that went begging and was ignored.

What did it feel like when you discovered that the one you yearned for and burned for felt the same as you? Your fire was their heat. How did it affect your thoughts? Your feelings? How did it affect your life? What was it like when you were together? What happened when you were forced to be apart? How did it affect your relationships with family and friends?

Take a minute to think about how this early love affair affected your life while I go and make us a pot of tea.

Did you do it? Come on now—I mean it. Take a couple of minutes and reminisce about a time you fell stark-ravingly, madly and badly in love. Now do it! Thanks.

Listening to hundreds of people talk about their early romances, a fairly universal pattern has emerged. Individuals from different countries, cultures, sexual orientations and generations come up with the same catalogue of experiences. For reasons that will be explained later, I call this pattern "lovesickness."

Symptoms Of Lovesickness

Euphoria

The first symptom of lovesickness is euphoria—that divine intoxication that rushes over its prey and leaves one weak, stunned and blissful. A delicious endorphin cocktail that produces both fever and delirium. For some, an exquisite numbness develops. Others tremble as their hearts leap and palpitate.

"I felt like I was stoned."

"I was floating on air."

For the newly smitten, spring is forever and flowers burst into resplendent bloom even if there's a blizzard blowing.

For some, the love-buzz may hit fast and furious, leaving its victim hopelessly love tossed; for others the intoxication takes weeks or even months to fully brew. This love-induced elation may be short-lived, lasting only minutes like a hit-and-run accident.

Comedian Richard Lewis put it this way: "When you're in love, it's the most glorious two-and-a-half days of your life." Compared to most drugs sold on the street today, this is quite a bargain if you can find it.

As told in the Old Testament, about 6,000 years ago, a lovesick king of Israel proclaimed, "How much better is thy love than wine" (Song of Solomon, 4:10). Today, due to advances in our understanding of the brain and its chemistry, we know that Solomon was onto something. The brain, after all, is a magnificent system of living chemicals which is equipped with, among other things, the ability to produce intense pleasure. The highs produced by alcohol and all the other mood-altering drugs depend largely upon the reward systems of the brain. Cocaine does not produce euphoria. Not really. Cocaine simply tickles the chemical systems that were there all along.

Later we will flesh out the love/drug connection. Right now, we are in love and have no time for such long-winded analysis.

Craving

There's no denying that the lovesick are under a sorcerer's spell. When together, young lovers are forever attempting to merge with their other half. Even those younger ones who have not yet discovered the alchemy of sex are consumed by this natural impulse. Despite the disapproving eyes of parents and society, young lovers are compelled to maintain constant contact with each other lest any separation break their divine circuitry. It is as if the two darlings are drawn toward each other by some supernatural magnet that would tear their respective hearts into pieces if it were resisted—not that they want to.

Inevitably, occasions arise that require them to separate, at least temporarily. Their happy symbiosis must come to a temporary end. After a great many goodbyes, so-longs and I'll-miss-you-so-muches, the lovers take their reluctant leave. Almost immediately upon parting, a bittersweet yearning begins. Only the afterglow of having just been in each other's company makes separation tolerable. In time, however, as the minutes spent in exile turn into hours, the longing for the absent other intensifies. He smells his clothing hoping to capture the remnants of his lover's scent; she hugs her pillow trying to cheat reality of its bitter truth—it will be nine hours until she sees her loved one again!

Finally, if the separation is unbearably prolonged—that is, for more than a day or two—the hours that precede the reunion are exquisite torture. Knowing that their hunger will soon be satisfied, the sufferers can no longer restrain their intense yearning. Damning the sluggish movements of the clock, each one's soul paces as if it were a tiger trapped in a cage.

Obsession

When in love, the only practical use for the mind is to think, dream and fantasize about the missing mate. Any other thoughts are worthless distractions. Regardless of which mental task is pressing for attention, the mind of the love-struck always has other ideas—and all of those ideas involve you-know-who.

A potent source of obsessions are those "sweet nothings" lovers hotly whisper before parting. "I'm going to miss you so much." "I can't wait to see you again." "Oh baby, I've never felt like this before." For the lovelorn suitor (or suitee), these sweet incantations serve as highly effective euphoriants. The mind need only call them to consciousness to gain a brief respite from the pain of separation.

Of all the phrases that get played and replayed in the sequestered lovers' minds, the first declarations of "love" hold a special status. "I love you, I love you, I love you." Is there any expression for which the spirit hungers more? "I love you." When in love, you can neither say it enough nor hear it enough. Despite a thousand repetitions, its lyrical simplicity is never tiring. "I love you, I love you, I love you." This is the pure stuff—it goes right to the core.

The obsessions of lovers do not depend exclusively upon things that are spoken. Infinite numbers of gestures, sighs, smells, touches and intonations are all remembered in exquisite detail. Then there are the questions: "Does he love me?" "Does he REALLY love me?" "Does she love me as much as I love her?" A field of daisies does not have enough petals to accomodate a lover's fevered fears: "She loves me; she loves me not. She loves me. . . ." Whether the relationship is going well or poorly, the lovers' minds drift unceasingly to what the loved one did, is doing or will do next time they're together. The mind has a mind of its own.

Protecting The Relationship

One of the hallmarks of this kind of love is the intensity with which the lovers work to protect it from outside threats. When friends or family criticize the relationship, the lovesick lover becomes defensive, even angry. "You don't understand; it's not like that at all," is the common refrain of the love-struck defendant. Should parents impose restrictions that interfere with a teenager's ability to see his or her current crush, the reaction can often be dramatic. In some cases, it is taken to tragic extremes, as in Shakespeare's "Romeo and Juliet." As you no doubt recall, Western literature's most famous couple end up killing themselves just because their parents said "no."

Another powerful manifestation of trying to protect the relationship is jealousy. Here the insecure lover begins to doubt the fidelity of the loved one, and his doubts poison both the relationship and every waking moment of his increasingly miserable existence. The jealous lover attempts to possess and control the loved one, trying to make sure that the partner will never stray. Frustrated at not being able to control the lover's actions or thoughts, the jealous one becomes obsessed with the imagined unfaithfulness. These dire ruminations often ripen into accusations and prosecutions. "Where were you on the night of . . . ?" The end result, of course, is to drive away the person they want so urgently to possess; the beloved hostage escapes.

Distorted Reality.

"Love is blind," goes an old joke, "and marriage is an institution for the blind." A lover's warts, moles, birthmarks and other physical flaws—not to mention a less than lofty IQ or a spiritual shallowness—can't be seen when you are gazing lovingly at them through rose-colored glasses. From an evolutionary point of view, our species probably depended upon us not being too circumspect in selecting mates—he who hesitates too long remains a bachelor (or bachelorette). A little distortion may help to ease negotiations between the two as they contemplate becoming as one.

It's worth pointing out, though, that reality exists for a

reason. While the long-term goals of evolution may be best served by this temporary psychosis, the parties involved frequently live to regret their sweet delusions. "If only I knew then what I know now!" That's the sad complaint of nearly everyone heading to divorce court.

Family and friends commonly attempt to awaken lovesick victims from their opiated dreams. These well-meaning efforts, however, are almost always resented. Woe to family members or friends who charge in and attempt to take matters into their own hands. Too often the dreamers only burrow deeper into their blissful coma and dismiss the intruders' entreaties as unfair, mean or just plain wrong. In fact, the lovers' commitment to illusion may be so complete that they forbid any and all persons from ever raising another cautionary note. Thus insulated from reality, our young lovers skip merrily, merrily, merrily along from mirage to marriage.

Building Your Life Around Your Loved One

Lovesick lovers do everything in their power to keep the relationship secure and on a steady course. This is understandable; they've never ever felt so wonderful, spectacular and delightful in their whole life. Consequently, every spare (and unspare) moment must be coordinated with the schedule and whims of the beloved. Family activities that were once enjoyed are now scorned if they conflict with a planned telephone call. Vacations and college selections are determined by how they fit into the love affair or whether they can be used to maintain the relationship.

Similarly, crucial issues like whether to wear blue jeans or a suit and whether to listen to classical or folk music are determined by the preferences of the perfect other. The psycho-logic goes something like this: a) I want her to love me; b) she likes heavy metal music; c) therefore, if I listen to heavy metal music she will continue to like me.

When taken to the extreme (as it often is), the lovesick victims abandon their own values and identify with their partner's. "He thinks, therefore I am." The merger of identities occurs unconsciously and without any open or conscious negotiation. The lovers depend upon telepathic channels; they can read each other's mind. Like primitive tribesmen attempting to divine the will of their local god, the lovesick often adopt bizarre conclusions about what will be pleasing. She changes the color of her hair because she hears him praise a blonde actress. He squares his shoulders and lifts weights because she admires her muscular dad.

When their false god proves to have feet of clay and the relationship comes to a bitter end, the results can be devastating. Whether or not the feeling is mutual, the emotional rug has been pulled out from under the lovers. The more he exchanged his identity for what he supposed would secure his idol's acceptance, the more he now feels violated and cheated. Ditto for her. But we're getting a little ahead of ourselves, talking about breakups and all—we're still in love.

Emotional Dependence And Social Isolation

Question: How can you tell that a friend has fallen in love?

Answer: You don't hear from her.

Question: How can you tell when her relationship is breaking up?

Answer: Your phone rings.

Lovesick couples form an exclusive bond that is self-sufficient for them—they've got each other and what more do they need? Degree by degree, this one relationship takes the place of all the other relationships they once enjoyed. As a consequence, old friends are neglected or even jettisoned. Wrapped in a comfortable cocoon of their significant other's acceptance, no one else is needed. Everything else is simply an interruption.

"As long as I've got you, I don't need anyone else." This sentiment might not always be spoken but it is almost always felt. The love of that one person is more precious than what anyone or anything else has to offer. When things go wrong, it is the boyfriend or girlfriend who is immediately turned to for support, comfort and assurance. The chill of a hostile world simply melts away when lovesick lovers are wrapped in each other's arms. As a result of this emotional dependency, the lovesick couple becomes increasingly isolated from the rest of humanity.

The French have an expression *folie de deux* (madness of two) which nicely summarizes this phenomena. The "mad" couple often become so isolated that their madness goes untested and they increasingly find it harder to fit in with the rest of the world. They retreat further and further into their cocoon-built-for-two. This two-member cult forms its own autonomous society, removed from the world and happy to stay that way.

Sacrifice

One of the ways that lovers demonstrate their devotion to each other is by making sacrifices. These sacrifices come in a number of forms but ultimately can be categorized as sacrifices of time, money and attention. Initially, these sacrifices are made gladly because of the pleasure the relationship brings. What better use of money, time and attention than to lavish them upon the object of our love? Because these sacrifices are made by someone under the influence of love, they are often made recklessly. Their heart is writing checks that their bank account can't back up.

The custom of giving an engagement ring and other gifts is partly an institutionalization of the notion that sacrifice is evidence of true love. The element of sacrifice can be found in courtship rites throughout history and all around the globe. Giving beyond one's means is a sign of commitment and heartfelt devotion. Indeed, Don Juans of every culture have exploited this code and bedded many an unsuspecting maiden through real or feigned sacrifice.

The Buzz Fades

Remember the exhilaration you felt the first time you held your honey's hand? How precious. What joy and delight. Or how about the first time you kissed the star of your dreams? Remember how time stopped and all cares dissolved as you melted together into a hot tangle? Didn't you feast upon lips and mouths, both devouring and merging at the same time? Oh yeah. The hours sprinted by and before you knew it, it was 3AM and you had some explaining to do to your parents.

Then what happened? After a few weeks or perhaps months, passions began to cool. Sure, there was still a nice high, but it did not quite reach the same feverish pitch that was once there. Maybe you discovered that you could keep the heat turned up by progressing through greater levels of intimacy: from first holding hands, then kissing, fondling, sex play and, finally, intercourse. With the passing of each new landmark in intimacy, the previous one tended to lose some of its charm, spice and fire.

Hand-holding is usually the first to go. Curiously, long-term lovers who have lost their way may choose to continue holding hands in order to demonstrate to themselves and others that they do still in fact love each other. Now it is a choice or habit, but not a compulsion.

The loss of the "love buzz" is a sneaky process, sort of like the loss of youth. You have no idea that the calamity is occurring until one day you find graying hairs or a face full of fine wrinkles staring back at you from the mirror. Similarly, the descent from the heights of love goes unnoticed until you discover that you have already bottomed out. There is *amour* no more. One day you're simply not looking forward to seeing the other person as much as you did in the past—you want some "space." Petty annoyances mount. Arguments come more easily. Indifference settles in.

Whatever the neurochemistry of the process, in time the furnace runs out of coal, the burning embers turn into ash and the lovers begin debating which end of the toothpaste should be squeezed. No longer intoxicated by your partner's lips, you now notice the fetid odor of the afternoon's lunch. No longer stunned by her glance, you look elsewhere for stunning.

Budding lovers may be loathe to consider the possibility, but it is inevitable that the blazing infatuation will eventually cool down. The passion can't last. If it did, we would all drop out of high school and stay forever crazed in the back seats of our parents' Chevy.

Perhaps a switch goes off in the brain after the hormones have come to a full boil, and an announcement is made: "Okay, Mr. Endorphin, you're done now. Go back to on-call status."

Sooner or later the lovesick lover must come to terms with the ugly truth. The thrill is gone. The bird of paradise is really a pigeon. The buzz was.

The experience I have just described is exactly analogous to that of the alcoholic or other addict who develops a tolerance for his drug. Initially, the alcoholic gets an incredible high from just a few beers. Many recovering alcoholics will describe their early drinking daze in terms that are downright romantic: "From the very beginning, I loved everything about drinking." "Nothing ever made me feel so good." Yet, over the course of time, a chemical process kicks in that scientists refer to as "tolerance." You have have to increase the dose in order to achieve the same euphoric effect. A person who previously got gloriously high on three cans of beer now has to drink six cans to reach the same level of intoxication.

In exactly the same way, lovesick lovers need to increase their dose: from holding hands to kissing to making love to having sex to . . . ???

The Breakup

When either of the lovesick lovers realize that they're no longer in love, the breakup process may begin. But it doesn't necessarily affect both the same way. The emotional consequences for the person initiating the breakup tend to be very different from those experienced by the recipient of the news. For purposes of understanding lovesickness, I am going to focus upon the experience of being told "it's over."

Since I am sure most readers have never had the experience of being dumped, I'd like to take some time and describe in detail the acute and long-term symptoms associated with forced love withdrawal. If we can understand this experience, we can understand much of why people stay trapped in their destructive behavior patterns.

Love Withdrawal: Acute Phase

The news has been delivered. Whether it comes in person, over the phone or via the mail, a predictable series of symptoms are likely to follow.

First, there is shock. "This can't really be happening. No, I must have misunderstood. Oh my God, it's over." Even if there have been warning signs—fights, diminished passion, even talks about breaking up—when it finally happens, there's an unreality to it that takes time to settle in. In the extreme, the rejected partner maintains a profound denial which can last for years. Once it becomes clear that there will be no bargaining and the end is here, our focus shifts from our heart to our gut. Nausea—a sense that something is rotting inside. Putrid. In the extreme, people vomit. In this acute phase, nausea manifests itself as a loss of appetite. At a deep level of our consciousness, our body is saying: "I have lost a part of myself—I no longer need to eat. What's the purpose?"

The sudden recognition that our loved one has abandoned us brings with it the discovery that, somehow during the love affair, millions of tiny hooks had imbedded themselves inside our heart and soul—and now they're being ruthlessly torn out. Other symptoms associated with the acute phase of love withdrawal include sleeplessness, crying jags, rage, irritability, confusion, violent fits, self-abuse and even suicide attempts.

Love Withdrawal: Chronic Phase

Within a couple of days or weeks, our lovesick loners move into a longer and almost as painful phase of the condition. Whereas initially they had no appetite, now they turn to food to fill emptiness. Cookies in the car or cupboard, candies in the purse or desk drawer. Food becomes a companion and a minor gratification, but only minor. There really is no gratification to be found anywhere.

Just as appetite is disturbed, so is sleep. The bed is empty, the night is empty, and all todays and tomorrows seem equally empty. This is in stark contrast with the fullness of their romantic yesterdays. And it is with these memories that they fill their sleepless nights. Sometimes tearfully, scenes from the relationship are played over and over, examined and re-examined from every conceivable angle. Like clothes in a washing machine in which someone had forgotten to pour in the soap, the recollections go round and round but never lose their stain. This agitated phase of withdrawal is made worse if it is fueled by the past partner's infidelity or betrayal. This high-octane pain fills the nights with rage and plans for confrontation or revenge, played out in technicolor detail.

Eventually, one of three things tends to happen to the lovesick victims who have loved and lost.

The Radar Scan

Once some equilibrium has come about and the more acute pain of loss has been stifled, displaced or forgotten, lovesick individuals may begin to scan the horizon for a new partner. Like a kitten or puppy that wandered away from its mom, they desperately set about looking for a new lover to fill the void. As we will see later, because the radar is so often faulty, this strategy usually brings only more of the same. Despite admonitions from friends and family, and especially from themselves, they just can't seem to help it. They fall for the same "type" again and again. More will be said about this later.

Substitution

Another path often taken by lovesick losers suffering withdrawal is the adoption of an impersonal substitute. There are lots of options. Drinking, popping pills, smoking crack, marathon TV watching, shopping, working and having anonymous sex are some of the more common examples. In combination or individually, the lovesick are doing the best they can to kill the pain. As one might guess, this strategy is fraught with more troubles. Again, we'll explore this in future chapters.

Recovery

This is the least common response simply because most people don't know how to do it. In fact, most people are unaware that there is anything that will make them whole and better able to choose wisely in love. Chapters 4 through

9 describe the lovesick recovery process. But we're not ready for recovery, however. Not yet.

It's Habit Forming

Looking over the symptoms of lovesickness, you can't help but notice that these are the same symptoms normally associated with *all* addictive disorders. Alcoholics, drug addicts, compulsive gamblers, compulsive overeaters, sex-and-love junkies, compulsive spenders and hoarders, power and money maniacs, co-dependents—addicts of all shades and flavors—all relate to their "drug of choice" as if they were teenagers in love.

These parallels are more than just a curious coincidence. Lovesickness reflects a person's sense of worth. It manifests itself in a relationship between a predisposed person and anything that either a) removes that person's feelings of worthlessness and/or b) gives that person a sense of worth. Addictive substances and all compulsive behaviors become entrenched in the addict's life because they initially removed a sense of worthlessness or provided a false sense of worth.

Regardless of the particular substance or compulsion, addicts get hooked because of the extraordinary euphoria they experience from using their drug of choice. This spectacular high leads to a strong desire to repeat the experience. That's called craving. When the craving goes unsatisfied, obsession and compulsion begin to develop. Fairly soon, the love affair with the addictive substance builds, and they work to protect the relationship against all threats. Similarly, addicts build their life around their addiction because nothing else is as important. This emotional dependence leads to social isolation and a willingness to make whatever sacrifice is necessary in order to further secure the relationship. Money, time and attention are all freely given in exchange for time engaged in the addiction

As every addict knows, the high produced by those first few doses can never be recaptured, and finally, as time goes by, it becomes impossible to achieve any kind of satisfaction at all. The dose must be increased or some new combination must be tried. Regardless of how creatively alchemical techniques are applied, addicts are never able to re-experience the oceanic sense of oneness that those first few highs produced. This is called "tolerance." Uncomfortable, often excruciatingly painful withdrawal symptoms develop upon attempts to become abstinent. Withdrawal is followed either by relapse, substitution of one substance (or person) for another—or recovery.

Lovesickness is what is going on inside of the person regardless of the outward manifestation. Lovesickness is the subjective emotional and motivational reality underlying all addictive compulsive processes.

A person can have addictive relationships with a variety of substances, activities and people; in fact, this is typically the case. A woman who has an addiction to food may temporarily give up chocolate chip cookies, but coincidentally find her obsession with men intensifying. Or she finds that her craving for chocolate is "miraculously removed" when she falls in love (only to return to chocolate once the relationship goes sour).

Similarly, alcoholics quit drinking only to transfer their addiction to tobacco, coffee, meetings and work are so common that the pattern has become a cliché. While abstinence from alcohol is certainly a significant improvement, if they just leave it at that they will be experiencing only a fraction of what life has to offer. Abstinent lovesick individuals are still plagued by a chronic state of loneliness and lovelessness. Their intimate relationships, assuming that they have any, remain basically adolescent in character. They continue to have addictive relationships with other drugs and activities (tobacco, gambling, overeating and so on). More importantly, abstinence alone puts them perilously close to relapsing to their drug of choice. To secure their abstinence—and eventually to go beyond mere abstinence—the lovesickness must be addressed.

Lovesickness and Recovery

Lovesickness isn't just about addiction, at least, not as we commonly think of addiction. Remember when you said to yourself: "Boy, when I get that car (or job or house or promotion or lover or degree or inheritance or whatever), I will be happy." Come on, admit it. Everyone has done it dozens of times. Some "thing" was going to really make a big difference in our lives and then we would live happily ever after. What happened?

You got the car and you were blissful for about three days. Even if it ran trouble-free forever, it eventually became just a car. Likewise with all of the other examples. To the extent that you look toward some person, place or thing to make you feel worthy, lovable or complete, you are vulnerable to lovesickness.

Accomplishments can be like this, too. The artist is driven to complete her spectacular, award-winning painting. A lawyer is trying a precedent-setting case. Or a psychologist is writing his first book about lovesickness.

Each significant step toward the ultimate goal yields a quest-sustaining euphoria. Such driven individuals will be obsessed with their task and will desperately desire or crave its completion. They are miserable when their project is dragging along or going poorly. When extreme, such monomaniacal efforts may be criticized by loved ones who feel abandoned or who are concerned about their loved ones' imbalanced lives. Against such criticism, our crusader will defend his work along with the social isolation that his obsession has necessarily produced. Sacrifice is an unavoidable and time-honored price for most great accomplishments. Yet, once the momentous case is won, the groundbreaking book hits the bestsellers list or the painting wows the critics, what happens to our champion?

When "More" Is The Drug Of Choice

Lovesick champions don't retire or kick back and bask in the warmth of their accomplishments. Haven't you been paying attention? Accomplishment is the approval junky's syringe, and the particular accomplishment is his "dope." I recently overheard a member of Narcotics Anonymous say that his drug of choice was "more." And so it is for all lovesick addicts.

Who's Immune?

It would be a mistake to claim that everyone suffers from lovesickness. Probably.

Psychologists (such as myself) tend to develop biased views of humanity because we only work with people who are having difficulties. Consequently, we develop a warped perspective on humanity. We don't get to work with the fully evolved, enlightened, self-actualized masses. All 20 of them.

Though there are no studies on the subject, it is likely that there are some people who have little or no tendency for lovesickness. They are healthy, well-adjusted and content. Perhaps their desires are modest and therefore their excesses are few. These would be folks who, due to some biochemical good fortune, have an innate sense of contentment, peace and serenity. Lucky them.

I've seen such enlightened beings in the movies and I've read about them in science fiction and fantasy stories. I've also read theological and philosophical stuff by and about various gurus who, if they are truly as described, may fit the bill: they may indeed be immune to lovesick tendencies. My guess, however, is that in real life many are just people who have developed great "acts"—they have mastered a facade of enlightened detachment. Their actions frequently reveal that they are unhealthily attached to their acts and their ever widening sphere of spiritual influence.

On the other hand, there *are* those who have developed healthy adaptations to their lovesick tendencies. Through insight, therapy or perhaps even grace, they have escaped from the lovesick cycle. Because of personal experience, as well as my work with others, I know that such adaptations to lovesickness are quite possible. But recovery from any addiction is an ongoing journey, not a destination that one arrives at once and for all. There is no cure, only sometimes blissful and sometimes bumpy-but-peaceful co-existence with our lovesick selves.

The rest of this book is about how we can gently grow beyond being controlled by lovesickness, one infatuation at a time.

CHAPTER 2

Sources Of Lovesickness

(Author's note: If you are suffering from a pounding headache, you're not going to be particularly interested in reading about the causes of headaches—at least not while you're in pain. Likewise with lovesickness. The next three chapters describe the causes of lovesickness (Chapter 2), the various possible manifestations or outward expressions of lovesickness (Chapter 3) and some general ideas about what does and doesn't help in overcoming lovesickness (Chapter 4). If your interest in the subject is mostly academic or casual, then feel free to read straight through. If you're looking for advice, skip ahead to Chapters 5-9; at your leisure you can come back to these other chapters.)

Lovesickness is at the heart of the human condition. To a greater or lesser degree, all people experience it. There are certain unavoidable events in life that guarantee each of us will have a dose of it. There are vast differences, however, in the degree to which a person may suffer from lovesickness.

For some, it is no more than an amusing diversion during their adolescent years, a brief fever and nothing more. For others, it is the central defining theme of their lives, like a chronic incapacitating illness. Most of us fall somewhere in between. But even then, the fall can be quite painful.

What are the causes of lovesickness? Are we born with it or is it the result of some childhood trauma? Can we become lovesick even if we had decent parents or is bad parenting a necessary condition? And why is it that lovesickness dominates one person's life and merely breezes by another?

The short answer to these questions is simply that anyone who survives birth has enough reason for at least a touch of lovesickness. Lovesickness comes with the territory of being alive. To be born, to live and to breathe sets up a desire for love. But there is a difference between having an appetite and having a desperate hunger. It is the desperation that defines the pathological expression of lovesickness. From whence comes this desperation?

The following is a list of factors that contribute to the development of lovesickness. One factor may be more critical than another, depending on the individual. Most people are influenced by several of these:

- prenatal experiences
- birth trauma
- drug withdrawal at birth
- traumatic loss
- traumatic stress
- neglect, abandonment or abuse
- suppression and denial of self in childhood
- trials of the teenage years
- confused values

These lovesick factors are presented in the order of their appearance in life. This order is deliberate. Events that happen early in life are most likely to have the greatest effect on future development. Events that happen later tend to have less of an effect.

On the surface, of course, the hurts that are freshest in our minds offer the most plausible explanations for our present actions and difficulties. It's infinitely harder to understand how faintly remembered events of our distant past can have such a powerful effect on how we feel and what we do today. It's even harder for us to relate to influences that came about long before, during and shortly after our birth. These ancient and preconscious events of our own personal histories may be the most influential of all.

It's In Our Genes

During the past few years, the results of several studies have had profound implications for our understanding of lovesickness. It is clear that there is a genetic predisposition for diseases such as cancer, hypertension, obesity and diabetes. It also appears that there is a genetic influence on personality. If we hope to gain a full and accurate understanding of lovesickness, we have to know what the geneticists have to say on the subject.

Let's begin our genetics exploration by briefly reviewing some real basic concepts.

Over the course of thousands and thousands of years, certain human behaviors and traits have paid off and others have not. For instance, those of our ancestors who couldn't climb a tree tended not to live long enough to pass this trait on. They were eaten before reaching puberty. Some physical and psychological traits had survival value, others didn't. Of particular interest to us is the evolution of pleasure and reward systems.

Within each of our brains are chemical systems that produce intense feelings of pleasure or satisfaction when stimulated. When these chemical systems are disrupted, behaviors that formerly produced pleasure lose their pleasure-producing abilities. The best known of these chemical systems are those inhabited by endorphins. Less well-known, but at least as important, are the dopamine, serotonin and norepinephrine chemical reward systems. These chemicals, or neurotransmitters, are produced in the brain and released when we do things that nature likes to reward.

What are some of these things that nature smiles upon? If we think about biological processes that produce feelings of pleasure, we come up with a short list: eating when we are hungry, drinking when we are thirsty, sleeping when we are tired and having sex when aroused. All of these behaviors play essential roles in the perpetuation of the human species.

Nature's Rewards

Not coincidentally, all of these behaviors are necessary for the survival of the species. If we didn't eat, drink, sleep or reproduce, the species would be fossilized all too quickly. Consequently, these behaviors had to be rewarded in memorable ways. Nature correctly guessed that we humans would do just about anything for pleasure!

Some people are born with differences in the way their brain produces, metabolizes and releases these rewarding brain chemicals. At research centers around the world, scientists have studied these differences in laboratory animals and in humans. A thorough examination of this research is way beyond the scope of this book, but we can take a look at a few highlights.

In the language of the brain, lovesickness is a disturbance in the dopamine, endorphin and/or other related reward mechanisms. Internal, subjective experiences of the lovesick individual are due to these biologically based reward systems gone astray. And their functioning is, at least in part, genetically determined.

Let's consider some of the research on the genetics of alcoholism.

Researchers at Yale University have looked at the endorphin levels of young children of alcoholics after the kids were given a small dose of alcohol intravenously. As a comparison, the researchers also gave the same amount of alcohol to children of *Good Housekeeping* seal-of-approval nonalcoholics. The researchers found that the children of alcoholics, after being exposed to a small amount of alcohol, produced about three to four times as many endorphins as the *Good Housekeeping* kids (Sadock and Kaplan 1985).

This chemical, which is associated with pleasure and is basically activated for the purposes of reinforcing sex and relieving stress, was released in enormous supply to the children of alcoholics after their brains were exposed to alcohol.

This is very significant. It suggests that there's a genetic difference in how much pleasure a person gets out of drinking. For some, it's merely a nice, moderate high. For others, it's indescribably euphoric. For still others, it offers no pleasure at all.

Other studies have suggested that addicted individuals may be walking around with lower levels of endorphins than nonaddicted individuals. This would mean that their own natural ability to release endorphins in response to stressful situations, such as love loss or trauma, is impaired. For people with a reduced capacity to release endorphins, life would be much more stressful. Losses would be harder to cope with. Thus the need to find comfort through various endorphin-stimulating activities may be born. And what types of activities may these be? Drinking, drug use and other addictive actions.

It is not clear whether the endorphins, dopamine or some other reward chemical will prove to be the key to our understanding the biology of addictive behavior. Evidence is increasing, however, that the way the brain's chemical system behaves is determined or at least greatly influenced by genetics. Each and every one of those little cells in our brain has 46 chromosones—23 from our mother and 23 from our father—and some of them have very specific instructions for that brain cell. They tell it how to conduct itself, what kind of stimulation it should respond to, what kind to ignore and how much stimulation is needed to produce a response at all.

Some Are Needier Than Others

It appears likely that some people inherit a reward system that leaves them in a state of chronic neediness; they're just born with an emotional hunger. Something in them keeps repeating, "Feed me, love me, need me."

Everybody needs love and acceptance and belonging, but for some people love seems no more demanding than a preference; it's very nice, but they don't seem devastated when the flow of love gets threatened or interrupted. For others, love is a matter of absolute desperation. These are the lovesick.

One way to think about it is that some people need love like sunshine: Yes, you've got to have some sunshine in your life and it's a lousy day that doesn't have some sunshine, but a few gray days in a row isn't the end of the world. The lovesick, on the other hand, need love like oxygen. The lovesick have got to have it constantly and when there isn't enough (and there rarely is), trouble begins. The lovesick person looks for other ways to fill the void. These are the people who go through life in a perpetual state of emotional neediness. "Fill me! Love me! Need me!"

As very young children, you'll see them clinging to their parents fearfully; they grab hold of things—a favorite toy, a stuffed animal, a "security blanket"—and go into a panic when they lose them. They turn to various types of escape or pain-numbing behaviors, like rocking or banging their heads or sucking their thumbs, to cope with their neediness.

Extreme head-banging and rocking are common symptoms of autistic children. It is interesting to note that researchers are beginning to study abnormalities in the endorphin systems of autistic children; rocking and head-banging are being looked at as means for stimulating those systems. If there is a link, autism could be an addiction to one's own brain chemistry; autistic children are not connecting with the outside world because they've found ways like rocking and banging themselves that somehow release extraordinary supplies of endorphins.

Because each of us inherit biological differences in our brain's reward chemistry, each of us also inherits differences in the degree to which we are prone to lovesickness. While the dynamics of lovesick neurochemistry are not entirely clear, it is likely that a unifying theory of the biology of addictions and compulsive behaviors will soon emerge. When it does, endorphins and dopamine will play prominent roles. Because the production of these chemicals can be influenced by genetics, it is safe to say that lovesickness, too, is influenced by genetics.

Drug Withdrawal At Birth

Birth. As adults, we give little thought to our experience of being born; we tend to think of it as a simple and insignificant fact of life. Since we don't remember the experience we think it is unimportant. Yet, it is possible that experiences which occurred during and immediately after birth may have had a profound impact on the rest of our lives.

Recently, medical science has embraced a number of changes in how babies are delivered. The Lamaze method, underwater birthing, music, warmer rooms, not using forceps—all these are efforts aimed at easing the transition from total dependence on the mother to semi-independent life outside of the womb. Today, we see pictures of newborns actually smiling shortly after birth.

The experience of birth, however, is not always so pleasant. For some newborns there are serious complications: a shortage of oxygen, toxicity, premature birth followed by incubation, drug withdrawal. All of these conditions, and others, can set the stage for a difficult and traumatic entrance into life.

Newborns don't speak. We don't know what is on their minds. And since we have forgotten our own births, we can only guess what it is like to be born and go through infancy. It may be that nature imbues all newborns with sufficient preparation for birth, assuming that all is always well. More likely, however, is that the birth process varies in its eventfulness and significance in terms of future psychological development. For some, we have reason to believe, birth experiences instill the foundations for insecurity and distrust that last a lifetime.

Tiny Addicts

As an example, let's consider the millions of newborns who go through drug withdrawal upon being born. According to recent studies, approximately 20 percent of children born in major metropolitan areas have cocaine in their systems at the time of birth. A woman who is addicted to cocaine is passing that drug on to her unborn child in adult-size doses. Say the unborn baby weighs three pounds and Mom weighs 120 pounds. The dosage designed for Mom to get high sends the baby spinning inside its mother's womb for hours. Often these babies die before being born; others die at birth or within the first few months. Some are deformed and some have serious developmental and psychological disabilities.

Obviously, for these unborns and newborns, life is dangerous and painful. The experiences of thousands of infants whose mothers are addicted to alcohol, heroin and other addictive substances follow a similar course of intoxication, withdrawal and trauma.

Babies Hooked On Nicotine

Let's toss our net a little wider. Consider the legions of babies who spend their first months of independent life craving a cigarette. As with their fellow babies who were exposed to the so-called hard stuff while waiting to be born, nicotine babies also go through a disturbing and painful withdrawal.

The facts are startling. Of some 47 million tobacco smokers, about half are women and more than half are of childbearing age. Consequently, every year thousands of children are born with a nicotine habit.

Babies absorb nicotine through the placenta and, as with cocaine, because of their comparative size they absorb nicotine at levels equivalent to several cartons of cigarettes a day. The unborn child is swimming in a sea of nicotine-filled amniotic fluid.

Numerous reports have been written about the health effects of smoking on the unborn child. You can even read about these effects on the sides of cigarette packs and cartons, as well as in the fine print at the bottom of the tobacco advertisements. Yet because Mom is hooked on a powerful drug, she smokes on. Even when she tries to quit, little help is available to her and her unborn child.

How does early exposure affect children and contribute to lovesickness?

After intoxicated babies are born, they immediately undergo drug withdrawal. Depending upon the substances to which they've been exposed, the withdrawal symptoms will be more or less violent and more or less traumatizing. Spending one's first days or months of life in drug withdrawal must be terrifying. During this critical period the infant's attention should be focused on a multitude of demanding developmental tasks such as bonding with the mother, feeding and improving visual acuity. For the thousands of infants undergoing drug withdrawal, another task presents itself: trying to cope with the loss of feelings associated with the mother's use of tobacco, marijuana, cocaine or whatever.

Though the infant has no concept of a cigarette, marijuana joint or whatever else the mother was using, it nevertheless is experiencing a strong craving for something. Something is missing! The infant craves for something but doesn't know what. Ironically, babies who are breast-fed will get some of the drug they're missing through their mother's milk! This can ease the withdrawal while perpetuating the drug dependency. Breast-fed or not, eventually the child will no longer be getting the drugs it has become physically dependent upon. When this withdrawal develops, the infant will experience what all addicts experience: *drug hunger*. Because this drug hunger takes place so early in life, however, the effects are more dramatic.

The brain of the unborn child grows very rapidly while inside the mother's womb. Then during the first year of life it doubles in size. From age one to age twenty-one it doubles in size one more time. If all this brain growth is occurring either under the influence of addictive substances or going through withdrawal from those substances, then it is likely that the basic architecture of the brain is going to be affected.

The substances we are talking about—nicotine, cocaine, alcohol, heroin, etc.—are taken specifically because of their ability to affect the chemistry of the brain. They are mood- and mind-altering substances. It is quite likely that frequent exposure to these brain-altering substances during the gestation period will permanently change the brain. In what way?

All of these substances act on the chemical reward or pleasure systems of the brain (dopamine, endorphins, etc.), and disturbances in the functioning of these chemical pleasure systems may serve as the basis for feelings of chronic deprivation and neediness. In other words: lovesickness.

Infants on drugs will grow into children, teenagers and adults who feel chronically needy, chronically missing something. Completely unconscious of the origins of this neediness, and unaware that this is an abnormal (or at least unhealthy) state of affairs, the emptiness will lead to a search for means of filling the void.

Culture, neighborhood and economics will influence the options that individuals turn to as they attempt to cope with their feelings of inadequacy. Some will turn to heroin, cocaine and alcohol. Others will settle for more socially acceptable options: tobacco, shopping and prestige. In either case, the deep down, in-your-gut, subjective experience is basically the same. The difference is one of degree, not kind. Both are lovesickness, an emptiness that begs to be filled.

Because most of us have no insight at all into the specific genetics or chemistry of our own brains and no conscious memories of the trauma of our birth or the pain of our first year of life, there's a tendency to want to fix all the blame for our lovesickness on what we do remember: trauma and abuse we may have experienced as a child. But it would be a mistake to do this. The biology of our brain's development plays a greater role in our destiny.

Parents Are Victims, Too

As we contemplate the hurts done to us, it may be worthwhile to consider that the reason Mom and Dad inflicted them upon us was that they themselves had little choice—something may have been passed on unknowingly from generation to generation. And you are just the latest in a long line of dysfunction.

To fail to recognize that our parents may be victims, too, helps to keep us stuck in resentment rather than moving us along in recovery. Recovery can't begin with anyone but you.

I am aware of people who have spent decades trying to undo their childhood abuse—decades trying to understand, forgive or, worse, remaining focused on condemning their parents or other abuser. Following this kind of path, although they are doing the best they can, may be a psychological dead end.

Unraveling the past is interesting; it's full of drama. Trying to learn what our parents were like and what they did, as well as how others may have influenced us, is engrossing. And to discover what happened to cause our parents to act the way they did toward us is even more fascinating and sometimes frightening. But no matter how far back or how thoroughly we search, in time it becomes clear that this is only a small part of the solution. It may even be a distraction that interferes with our taking responsibility for finding reliable sources of unconditional love. There is a risk of getting caught up in too much psychological archaelogy—digging up the past—and not enough focus on practical solutions for today.

The past can't be ignored. It's true—and we'll talk more about this later—that as part of the recovery process we have to get beyond our self-loathing and self-hate. To do this we need to detoxify ourselves or rid ourselves of emotional toxins from the past. John Bradshaw, author of *Healing The Shame That Binds You*, and others have done a good job of spelling out elements of this process (Bradshaw 1988). But this is not enough. In the long-term what you need are reliable sources of unconditional love.

Having said all that, let's consider the role of things like abuse, neglect and abandonment in the development of lovesickness.

Stunted By Neglect

Physical and emotional abuse actually can change the chemistry of the brain. The most startling example can be found in a well-documented medical condition called "psychogenic dwarfism." This condition, caused by parental abuse and neglect, is characterized by a dramatic stunting of a child's physical growth. A nine-year-old child will have the physical and mental development of a five-year-old. Interestingly, if these stunted children are removed from their abusive parents and put in a foster home, they grow physically and begin to develop cognitively.

In one of the standard medical textbooks, there's a picture of a psychosocial dwarf who's five years old but who has the height, 35 inches, of a two-and-a-half-year-old. The stunting occurs when the attachment of the child to the mother, a child's first source of love, is severely disturbed. As a result of the interruption of love from mother to child, there's a stunting of growth physically and, of course, socially and psychologically as well. Bonding and attachment are broken off.

Failure to thrive is another well-documented phenomenon associated with neglect. Children may be given enough food, but if they're not held or cared for emotionally, the basic physical need for love and connectedness isn't being met and that child's life is in jeopardy. Babies can die for love.

A key point, and perhaps the most important point about the role of early trauma, is that it causes physical, biochemical changes in the young person's brain. This is because everything that happens to us is stored in our brains as conscious, preconscious or unconscious memories. Everything. While specific details of inconsequential events tend to get blurred and blended into our reservoir of memories, the more meaningful events are given special status. We know that many animals with much smaller brains exhibit a memory skill called "one-trial learning": particularly *painful* conditions can be learned and avoided after only one exposure. Pain-producing circumstances are memorized after only one run-in.

Humans no doubt have a similar capacity to permanently store memories that are especially painful for future reference, even if they only occurred once. Thus, when a child is abused by a parent or any "caregiver," a template may be created chemically within the brain that makes relationships with future caregivers frightening. This translates into an adult who avoids any source of care or nurturing because of the often unconscious associations that were established by the early abuse.

Those individuals who are love-phobic are trapped in a serious bind. On the one hand they are fearful, avoiding people and situations that can lead to nurturing and love. On the other hand, their need for love is undiminished. In fact their need for love may even be quite extreme due to the chronic avoidance of what they need. As a consequence they, experience a chronic sense of neediness and love hunger. They are lovesick.

Getting The Bright Out

Consider the healthy, well-adjusted and well-loved child. Just look at that child's bright, lively eyes and natural curiosity which leads to exploring, spontaneously laughing and getting into everything!

Now, look at a child who has been abused. The curiosity and liveliness is gone or warped. The child is annoyed and annoying, disturbed and disturbing.

It's extraordinary that in so many cases what's considered normal childrearing is also a brutalization of the spirit. Parents do things to children that they would never consider doing to another adult. Sadly, many culture's norms include varying degrees of child abuse.

Children have few rights, few advocates and no recourse when faced with abuse. And we adults have been poorly educated about how we can do better.

When I was a young psychologist, I had the experience of working with emotionally disturbed children in a behavior modification program where all we used was "positive reinforcement." As behavior modification counselors we were trained to ignore inappropriate behavior and to reward the behavior which we were seeking. The children in the program were among the most disturbed kids in South Carolina; all of them had either been kicked out of elementary school or had simply dropped out. Despite incredible histories of truancy and mental illness, these kids went through the entire summer without a fight. One child went from near autistic withdrawal and another from sociopathic violence to become really super children.

Unfortunately, there is little education in general and very few social supports in our society to encourage parents to raise children in a healthy, loving and nurturing fashion. In the absence of good parenting education, we have exhausted, frustrated and horribly pressured parents resorting to physical and emotional coercion to achieve some semblance of control. All of us pay the price.

Mugging Kids

We pretend that a child doesn't feel the pain that an adult feels. Ironically, when we hear of an adult who's been mugged, it's a big deal. It makes the newspapers. Kids get mugged all the time, and it's not a stranger who mugs them but rather the person who's supposed to be protecting them.

As a therapist, I have listened in horror to client after client describing methods of torture they were subjected to by their parents. A father required his seven-year-old daughter to fetch the belt that he would use to beat her. A mother threatened to leave her five-year-old on the corner of a dangerous neighborhood at night. Smack! Whack! Because parents have been doing it for generations, we don't think anything of it. Such abuse drives a child to be fearful, distrustful and wary of others. In the extreme, such children will avoid others altogether. Isolated in this way, the need for love simmers and boils unsatisfied. The result is lovesickness in its many manifestations.

Denial Of Self

Related to abuse is the far more subtle and far more pervasive phenomenon called "denial of self." I remember in sixth grade some junior high school rock 'n roll band came to our school to perform. It was the first time I'd heard live rock 'n roll music. Well, the experience was fantastic. I was so moved by the music, I began rocking back and forth in my chair in the auditorium. I was having the greatest time! Unfortunately, other kids began making fun of me because I was "spazzing out." I was so embarrassed when they made fun of me that I stopped rocking back and forth and dancing there in my chair. In a tiny way, because of peer pressure I denied my feelings and killed off a portion of my natural self.

All of us all have experienced it. You walked into your seventh grade class wearing white socks. The unspoken code was that you were to wear only black socks; so you're the odd man out. Maybe you like white socks. Tough. Society says you wear black socks and so you "go along with the crowd."

The problem is that in the process of fitting in and learning to belong we are constantly denying ourselves; we are constantly saying "no" to our own inner sense of what is good and what is worthwhile. This denial of self is so subtle, most of us aren't aware of it when it's happening. But the longer-term effect is to become a phony actor whose socks, thoughts and beliefs all belong to someone else: them. By being so busy trying to fit in and belong, we forget what we actually like. Under these conditions, all of our interactions will have a tinge of artificiality to them. There's no direct contact with the world; we experience the world through a filter of "acts" or rules which we bought, one at a time.

Thus insulated, only the most pointed events can touch us. Intimacy is out of the question. Only the intensity of excess stimulates and touches us. Cut off from life in this way, our need for connectedness and personal closeness grows. In time, if uncorrected, the result may be a severe sense of loneliness, isolation and alienation. Lovesick, again.

The Trials Of Teendom

At some point—often in the spring—the call is heard. You wake up some morning and your soul is crying out: "Love me!" There's evidence that this is happening younger and younger, earlier and earlier. The desire to be accepted in a romantic way by somebody else is incredibly powerful. The human species counts on it. But it's something that the species hasn't entirely worked out yet. We have this incredible need, which becomes acute in adolescence, when the romantic urge appears. The hormones change and the desire to connect sexually with someone else reaches a feverish pitch. This chronic love neediness becomes so severe for most adolescents that at this time, if it hasn't already happened, we begin to see the outbreak of addictive behaviors.

Whether it's a sexual, romantic or gambling addiction; alcohol or drug addiction; or an eating disorder; it usually develops during these teenage years. Why? The thing teenagers want most is acceptance by a group and, romantically, by another person. It cannot be overemphasized how powerful a factor this is in a teenager's life and in the development of adult lovesickness.

What do addictive behaviors and lovesickness have to do with this? As we saw in Chapter 1, adolescent love affairs provide a perfect model for addictions; they serve as a template for understanding any kind of addictive behavior. Beneath all destructive compulsions is this desire to be loved, to belong and to be accepted.

It is no coincidence that addictive behaviors develop at the same time teenagers first experience the violent onslaught of hormonal changes. The teenager's subjective, internal experience of these libidinal stirrings is the essence of lovesickness.

Substances such as alcohol and drugs help the lovesick teenager address this new, startling experience because they help to remove inhibitions. Teens are desperate for a romantic relationship. But they are all afraid of rejection. Alcohol and drugs reduce their fear of being rejected. Athletics and politics are other ways of combatting rejection. Teenagers who play volleyball or football gain recognition and popularity, and are thus more apt to be liked. So are those who run for class office. High school quarterbacks and student body presidents hear roars of approval and get their names in print. But even such widespread respect and popularity is no assurance against rejection. Many people in the limelight are insecure when it comes to love.

Some people are extremely inhibited and shy. Besides, not everyone can be quarterback or class president. So many teenagers opt for drugs and alcohol. These substances reduce the fear of rejection by temporarily removing inhibitions. Addictive behaviors are a quick and dirty remedy for teenage lovesickness.

Some things, some actions can actually become love substitutes. They become a "lover" or "love object" in and of themselves. Some people, for example, are in love with their car. They give love to their car and imagine getting it back from their car; the car is not just a possession that's supposed to attract love but it also is the object of a primary love relationship. Before cars there were horses, and some people still have horses with which they have this primary love-substitute relationship.

Some kids go home and get wasted all by themselves; they're very lonely and the booze or the drugs serve as their best or only buddy. They may smoke a joint with another kid, but there's no interaction between the two of them except around that drug, and so the primary love relationship is with that drug. But it's not just alcohol or pot that can be a love object. The primary love relationship could be with a computer. Adults customarily would approve of that because it looks very constructive. But a child looking to a computer for love is going to have a "micro" personality down the road: comfortable around machines, estranged from people. Anyone who accepts a substitute for the real thing is in trouble.

Another connection between the teenage years and lovesickness involves the anesthetic or analgesic quality of various substances and activities. An insecure, lovesick teenager is going to find any thing or activity he can take, consume or engage in very attractive if it anesthetizes him, makes his brain numb, takes him out of himself or removes him from any consciousness of self. This is particularly true if he's an awkward kid who doesn't see any way of getting his love needs met. Heroin is a great anesthetic. Alcohol is a great anesthetic. Any substance that can create oblivion is bound to be popular. But so are compulsive shopping, marathon TV-watching, compulsive overeating and any other type of ritualistic behavior. Masturbation can become such a ritual. A teenager who engages in masturbation eight times in a day is doing the best he thinks he can to cope with his newly developed love neediness. He engages in this ritual to blot out the love neediness that keeps nagging at him. Anything that works may be repeated. Anything that works well is likely to become a pattern that continues into adulthood.

Starved For Attention

Some of these behaviors are attention getting. By drinking, by driving a sharp car or by supplying drugs at the party, the teenager can guarantee attention and status among his peers. Attention or recognition is a diluted version of the affection and love for which the teenager so dearly yearns.

At the behavior modification camp where I worked, the primary reward we gave was attention: pats on the back, eye contact, a smile. Amazingly, despite the severity of our clients' pathology, we were able to effect dramatic changes in their behavior. I was awed by how powerful attention is. Children are starved for attention. As Scott Peck pointed out in *The Road Less Traveled*, attention is an act of love (Peck 1980). It may be only a teaspoon of love, but we are starving for it.

Teenagers will do whatever is necessary to get attention. They get it by exceptional performance or poor performance, by acting enthusiastic or troubled. Society wants teenagers to do to positive, constructive things. While some of the so-called positive behaviors, such as absorbtion in computers, look good in the short run, they can have damaging long-term consequences. The negative ones are more obviously self-destructive but are immeasurably easier to do. All the teenager knows is that certain activities help to relieve love hunger.

The Worst Things In Life Are For Sale

Most of us are not as rich as the people we see on TV and in slick magazines. Yet the message we learn from these media is that your self-worth is dependent on your financial worth. If you don't have a whole lot of money, you're not worth much.

By that criterion, most people have zero or negative worth, because most people are in debt. This causes a feeling of inferiority that becomes especially severe among the large portion of our planet that is living in poverty, particularly in Western cultures where you can very easily compare yourself to the guys and gals on TV who look sharp, dress sharp and have innumerable glitzy possessions. A prime example: the inner-city kid who sees nothing in his neighborhood that compares with the great wealth portrayed on TV.

What that inner-city kid doesn't know, or hasn't been told, is that even if he had the possessions, it wouldn't cure his feeling of worthlessness, which is a symptom of lovesickness. Possessions, as well as addictive substances, can be poisonous when we use them to try and fill the basic human need for love. Designer clothes or a new car can't satisfy love neediness. The relief brought about by acquiring coveted possessions is only temporary. Much of our society is on this treadmill. How stupid can we be to think that the latest model toaster oven is going to bring us peace of mind?

A new trinket or a new toy are things that can only momentarily make us feel more lovable. Strange, isn't it? It's like that new car smell. It and the hey-look-at-me-feeling that comes with it are soon gone.

The truth is: There are things in life that are truly beautiful, and they will fill the void within ourselves, but none of them are for sale.

The things that cannot be sold are what we need the most: love of self, love of God and a relationship with a loving community. Not only can't you buy these things, but the degree to which money enters the picture is the degree to which love moves out!

For example, to the degree that money enters into a relationship with God, the relationship becomes false and is made impure and conditional. If I believe I am loved for my money, I can't enjoy the comfort of love. I may enjoy sex, I may experience closeness, I may be given compliments, but they are predicated on my money, not on me. These things don't reach my inner self.

No one can make a buck from unconditional love; as soon as love is for sale it becomes conditional and the healing properties evaporate. Twelve-Step fellowships such as Alcoholics Anonymous work, at least in part, because they're free. Although this may go against the tenets of our free-enterprise, capitalist system, if somebody is making money in helping you, it's going to be less effective than if the help were freely offered.

The values that are reinforced in our society, the things that we get hit over the head with on a daily basis on billboards, in magazines, on television, at work, are all about money. As a result, we end up believing that what's most important in life are things that can be bought and sold. We have to have more. More, more, more.

Movie theaters are packed; they're building more movie theaters all the time. Why? We need more places to go to escape from our emptiness, to distract us from our emptiness, because we're essentially empty, because we're trying to fill ourselves with stuff that doesn't fill us and that won't stick to our spiritual ribs.

The success of 12-Step fellowships is predicated upon giving without expectation of return, without concern about what's in it for me. Ironically, people hooked on addictive substances are self-centered and immature in the extreme, but they are able to maintain sobriety and become constructive members of society through selfless service that doesn't cost a penny.

Fish don't notice the water they swim in and we don't tend to realize that our birthrights have been sold by the quest for more, bigger and newer!

Breakdown Of The Family

In the history of our species, two institutions have played an important role in helping to fulfill the need for love: the family and religion. I harbor no romantic notions about the good old days. In many ways, these institutions have resorted to barbaric methods for self-preservation. Today, partly because of the brutalities practiced by many families and religions, these institutions have been challenged and undermined. They have been transformed from essential cornerstones of society to optional or irrelevant ingredients.

Fewer children are growing up in the traditional family of two biological parents plus siblings. There are broken, blended, foster and single-parented families. Similarly, organized religions are experiencing a dramatic downturn in attendance and financial support. Unfortunately, in the absence of these two institutions, humans are experiencing unprecedented turmoil.

We need to feel grounded in a loving family that fulfills our emotional needs. Without a stable family connection, we feel separate and adrift in an uncaring and hostile world. Many of us have difficulty trusting others because we have had few positive experiences in trusting. Unfortunately, this makes fulfilling one's love needs very hard.

Likewise, to the degree that we have been hoodwinked by, abused by or made afraid of organized religion, we will have a tainted and toxic view of God and spirituality. When I was six or seven years old, I was shown films about the Auschwitz and Dachau concentration camps. I was told about little Jewish boys being tortured by the Nazis, how they were killed and turned into lamp shades and bars of soap. I came to see God as someone who a) didn't much care for the Jews, and/or b) wasn't doing His job as God very well.

My experience is not unique. I have heard numerous stories from patients and friends who have had far worse experiences in the name of God through physical assaults, seductions and emotional torture. Small wonder, then, that when given the freedom to choose, many people run away from religion.

The desire to belong to some group with whom one can identify is ancient and very strong. It may even be a basic biological drive inherent in our psychological makeup. People need something to believe in, place their faith and trust in and build or organize their life around. When the family is lacking, people will create something of their own, either through formal means such as marriage or informal means such as drinking buddies, poker pals, casual sex partners or other pseudo-intimacies.

A tarnished image of God does not keep people from searching for divine blessing. In the absence of healthy spirituality, people will settle for a distilled version. Alcohol or drugs become a kind of holy sacrament that is imbibed religiously. Cheers!

The spiritual void can be filled by absolutist cults. The need to feel loved, accepted and to belong is part of who we are, and if we don't find a healthy, positive means for satisfying this need, alternative pathways will be discovered.

Embedded in being human is the desire, and the need, to be loved and to belong. Unfortunately, very few of us have developed adequate lifestyles and life strategies for finding the love we need.

CHAPTER 3

Lovesickness And The Addictions

The roots of the word "addiction" go back to the time when Roman armies were conquering the known universe. When a Roman general had succeeded in taking over a neighboring territory, the conquered soldiers and citizenry were brought before him for sentencing. The general pronounced his new subjects to be slaves. That sentencing was called an "addictum"; the "addicts" were bound and forced into slavery.

It wasn't until the 1600s that the word "addiction" lost its original meaning and was first applied to a substance: wine. Hardly eye-popping now, it was quite a revelation back then: Wow, a person could be enslaved to wine!

Addiction is no longer used in the original sense of the word, but it ought to be. When a person is addicted, the object of the addiction calls the shots. Perhaps obediently, perhaps grudgingly, the person does what the addiction commands. He or she is, in fact, a slave.

It is generally agreed among members of 12-Step fellowships and many professionals in addiction work that for something to be considered an addiction, two elements must be present: powerlessness and unmanageability.

The concept of unmanageability is easy to understand; it simply means that the activity or substance makes a person's life a mess.

The concept of powerlessness is more subtle. Powerlessness doesn't mean that addicts have no control over themselves, although that's sometimes the case. More precisely, it means that they have no control over what their *mind* is doing. Their mind has a mind of its own.

Despite cocaine addicts' sincerest intentions, their minds will say, "Geez, let's go back to that crack house and smoke up next week's paycheck." Or fitness addicts will say, "Geez, a ten-mile morning run will be nice; no need to worry about those shin splints; they don't hurt so bad anyway."

Returning To The Scene Of The Crime

Addicts' minds have a strong tendency to return to the destructive, addictive behavior again and again. A yearning followed by a rationalization leading to action. Powerlessness over certain thoughts leading to behaviors that make life unmanageable.

Here's a five-word definition that is a bottom-line indication of whether something's an addiction: "Continued use despite serious problems." If a person keeps on doing something that causes serious problems time and time again, then it is an addiction. The greater the problem, the worse the addiction.

The definition of what isn't an addiction is: those things that enhance an individual's well-being, that contribute to a fulfilling life. At the very least, they do not cause damage to the individual's life.

When I was a graduate student, I spent a lot of time studying and working because I had a specific goal in mind: to get a Ph.D. in psychology. I was thinking constantly about my dissertation and my exams. Other things took a back seat in order to achieve that long-term goal. This is called delayed gratification; the behavior enhanced my well-being and it wasn't destructive, even though I was clearly obsessed.

Similarly, when an Olympic athlete has a particular goal and pursues it in an obsessive manner, other areas of his or her life may be subordinated or even damaged in the pursuit of the "gold." If in the pursuit of this goal, the athlete's well-being is enhanced, we would say he is doing a healthy, positive thing. On the other hand, if the workouts, the training schedule and the lifestyle are making the athlete's life a mess or not enhancing the athlete's well-being, and he continues anyway, we would say there's something else going on here. It begins to look very much like addiction.

It is important to emphasize that addiction always involves repetition of some destructive behavior. Anyone can repeat a mistake once or twice. Anyone can get drunk and drive after a wedding and have an accident. Stupid, yes, but not necessarily an addictive act. The arrest doesn't make him an alcoholic. If, on the other hand, he keeps on doing it, and if he feels compelled to keep on doing it even though the evidence reveals that it's repeatedly wrecking his life, then we'd say it's an addiction.

Let's say that our Olympic hopeful is falling apart. He is taking steroids to become stronger. Or, in the case of a female gymnast, she is starving herself and literally stunting her growth to try and remain the optimum size for that sport. Even though the goal being pursued is one that society values, we should suspect addiction if our athlete feels compelled to compete despite the fact that his or her life is disintegrating.

Many addicts achieve things we applaud. Classic examples can be found in the writers Poe, Coleridge, Faulkner, Hemingway, Fitzgerald, Sinclair Lewis and Thomas Wolfe, all of whom were alcoholics or addicts. Their works have enhanced our understanding of the human condition, and have entertained, enlightened and broadened our perspective on life. Yet all of them were destroyed by their addictions.

How Does It Pay Off?

Some would argue that their addictions were also their genius—that the alcohol and drugs inspired the writing. Not so. In making a diagnosis of addiction, we're not concerned about whether it pays off for society, but whether it pays off for the individual.

It's not just obsession plus failure that equals addiction; obsession plus success can add up to addiction, too. Say you're that Olympic athlete and you win the gold medal. You've got a million-dollar endorsement contract from Wheaties, but if you're not able to enjoy it, if there's no joy or satisfaction in your life, what good is it? That's the dilemma for addicts. Those who express their addiction through achievement believe (in psychological shorthand): "If I achieve these things, I'm going to be more lovable." The day they win the gold medal is the greatest day in their life . . . and three days later they are despondent and have no idea what to do next.

Delayed gratification is a healthy process. It's when gratification is delayed forever or the price is so exorbitant that it becomes unhealthy. Pursuit of conditional love—if I succeed I'll be loved—is only going to produce conditional, short-term benefits. Such strategies always require another fix, dose or "more, more, more."

Are there better or worse addictions? Here, we get into the dimensions of addiction. In evaluating addictions and understanding the manifestations, one of the aspects we should look at is toxicity or pathology. How many problems does the activity cause? How rapidly is the damage done?

Some addictions create a greater pathology than others. Some can kill you very quickly, some take a long time to do their worst. Exercise addiction is generally not as toxic as crack cocaine addiction. The work addict doesn't create as much toxicity as the person who's a compulsive gambler. Unmanageability varies from one addiction to another. Substance addictions tend to produce more toxicity than behavioral addictions. Yet even with these there are differences.

Compulsive overeaters can die from gorging, but death comes slowly. They're subject to social ridicule, to insidious health problems and discrimination. Obesity dramatically affects their self-esteem. It can affect their ability to progress in their job. The barbituate addict, on the other hand, can have a fatal seizure or convulsion, or can overdose on any given day. The barbiturate addict lives constantly on the brink of shattering like a sheet of glass.

Admired Addictions

Some addictive behaviors are highly pro-social. Society is perfectly happy to see people destroy their lives in the pursuit of society's values. We have the compulsive worker who rises to the top of the corporation but whose personal and emotional life is a wasteland barren of any joy or satisfaction. Yet he is widely admired.

At the other end of the extreme are those whose addictions are highly stigmatized, such as crack or heroin addicts who turn to prostitution or burglary to support their addiction. As a society, we're more comfortable calling them addicts because they don't contribute much to society. With them, it's not so much a diagnosis as it is an accusation. It's not a disease, it's a disgrace. So we tend to differentiate between addictions according to stigma. If it causes problems for society, it's an addiction; if it causes problems only for the individual, it's not.

We don't tend to think of watching television or shopping as addictive because everyone does it. Besides, it doesn't cause us any problems if someone watches the tube twelve hours at a stretch. Or does it?.

Under the skin and in the heart, the compulsive shopper and the crack-head have more in common than most people think. Both do what they do because it stimulates their own reward systems in the brain, and any behavior that stimulates those brain chemicals has the potential to become an addiction.

Compulsive overeaters binge on certain foods, compulsive gamblers bet it all on one roll of the dice and compulsive workers put in 80-hour weeks because, in each case, doing so triggers brain chemistry that makes them feel good or keeps them from feeling bad.

Ultimately, the reckless pursuit of these addictive behaviors is to soothe an emptiness that stems from lovesickness. That's what all these addictions have in common. Why some people get involved in one pattern of behavior and some in another is determined by culture, values, personal history, family history and genetic differences.

Let's look at some of the more common adictions and examine how they are related to our need for love.

TV Addicts

Sitting alone in their apartment, a remote in one hand and a bag of chips next to the other, TV addicts surrender their lives to a 19" diameter world of soap operas, talk shows and movies. In the extreme, they can't work because they can't tolerate the thought of giving up all those mesmerizing shows.

For these addicts, the drug is strictly electric. The trials and traumas of others are the balm and euphoriant which television junkies shoot up every day. They don't take a vacation unless they can watch television. The real people in their lives and their own trials and traumas are overwhelming. Those troubles are tiring, annoying and depressing. But with just the slightest push of a thumb, they can slip into other worlds and other lives, leaving personal troubles far behind.

TV addicts steal to support their habit. They don't necessarily turn to prostitution or burglary to pay their electric bills. The addiction simply robs them of life. Hardcore TV addicts are no longer players in life, they're just observers, and it's not even real life they're observing. They take little but contribute little as well. They sneak off into their fantasy life and ask that the rest of us be quiet and leave them alone until a commercial break.

Alone? Far from it. They've got dozens of friends who visit daily. These friends don't make a mess and the only demand they make is to "stay tuned 'cause we'll be right back."

The addiction begins for many in early childhood. Parents discover that television is a superb baby-sitter and entertainer. "Go watch TV," says Mom. As science fiction author Harlan Ellison dubbed it, TV is the "glass tit." It amuses, it soothes, it gives children the "attention" parents seem unable to give. And, of course, the child does not seem to mind.

All in all, it seems like a fair enough deal: with so many demands on parents today, what's wrong with allowing a child to watch TV?

More recently, video games have been added to the mix; this makes the escape from reality even more thorough by adding an interactive element to it. This interactivity draws the viewers deeper into the television world. Their skills in controlling the video characters are refined and fine-tuned to razor precision. In absolute safety, the video game participant can kickbox, play basketball, slay demons from other worlds and defend the planet. Harmless stuff? Maybe.

Just like other addictive substances, TV can be used or abused. It can also become a destructive dependency. When a person is compelled to watch TV; when there's a sense of obligation or necessity; when choice is diminished and "want to" really means "have to," then we have an addictive process.

TV addicts use televison as a love substitute. Loneliness, intimacy and companionship are banished day and night.

Compared to other addictions, television addiction is a relatively harmless one. Still, there is a price. What is particularly significant about TV addiction is that it is so pervasive: 98 percent of American households have at least one television set, making TVs more common than telephones! As the number of channels multiplies, and as interactivity becomes more available, there is a strong possibility that still more people will retreat into video unreality or virtual reality. Estranged from each other, people spend hours gazing at television, but not a second into another's eyes.

Only Humans Like Smoke

When it comes to addictions, no substance is more illustrative of the problem than the killer of hundreds of thousands and the drug of choice of tens of millions more: nicotine.

Humankind's ingenuity in finding habits to carry to extremes is infinite. We are the only species that pursues smoke, as opposed to running away from it. We pursue it despite the fact that when we first use it, it isn't pleasant. It does not produce euphoria. In fact, the first reaction to drawing smoke into one's lungs is usually a combination of nausea, gasping, choking and coughing. Not to mention dizziness. But we're smart. We figure out that to prevent these symptoms we must smoke more, not less. So we smoke until we're hooked.

Being addicted to nicotine has one significant advantage. Every time we light up, we avoid uncomfortable nicotine withdrawal. This provides a pleasant sense of relief and satisfaction—the same kind you get from taking an aspirin. The pleasure smokers talk about is mostly relief from withdrawal symptoms!

Lovesickness makes people start smoking. Smoking makes youngsters feel sophisticated, attractive, grown-up; it gives them a sense of belonging and of being lovable. Cigarettes are chemical connections with other people; you borrow and share cigarettes with friends. It's a pseudo-intimate transaction. And when alone or lonely, a cigarette is a companion.

Despite all the negative press and social pressures against it, smoking is increasing among women. What are the motivations? One is the desire to be slim. Nicotine is an anorectic. It reduces the appetite and speeds up metabolism, helping women to become or stay thin. And why do women want to become thinner? Yup, so they can be more attractive and loved.

While the need for love and belonging is behind the initial use of nicotine, once a person continues to use it the chemistry of the body begins to change. Withdrawal occurs in the absence of use. Looking cool is no longer the motive; avoiding pain is. A permanent alteration of the nicotinic receptors in the brain occurs.

People whose chemistry was changed in the womb of their smoking mother prior to birth may be more likely to become addicted in later life. Nicotine was in their bloodstream at birth, in their mother's milk and finally in the air they had to breathe.

In addition to the craving caused by altered brain chemistry, other cravings are caused by learned behaviors associated with smoking—the nervous tamping, the constant flicking of ashes, the deep drag and the sigh that follows. When people feel particularly stressed, alone, isolated, unloved and unlovable, they are more apt to revert to behaviors that worked for them in the past. That's when they're going to light up.

Other associative links trigger the brain reward system. Nicotine is a stimulant and so is caffeine. The two stimulants augment or enhance each other. Then there's the proverbial cigarette after sex; nicotine augments reward systems there, too.

That's how our reward systems are patterned and conditioned. We are hard-wired to seek pleasure, so any behavior that enhances pleasure is learned at a deep and unconscious level. We're like Pavlov's dog, one behavior triggering another. Research has shown that if heroin addicts undergoing withdrawal see a syringe, they begin to sweat and their body temperature rises. These are learned cues that were conditioned into addicts' minds through repetition. Addictive behaviors are associated with certain paraphernalia or props.

If one is used to smoking while talking on the telephone, a ringing phone triggers the desire for a cigarette.

Nicotine chewing gum and the nicotine patch may be useful in helping an addict quit smoking. But for settling one's nerves, the gum and the patch can't compete with actual smoking. The gum and the patch don't involve lighting a match, taking that first initial powerful puff or sucking that smoke into the body. There's no enjoyment in blowing a smoke ring or in watching smoke curl lazily toward the ceiling. There's nothing to just hold in your hand. Nothing to satisfy the lovesickness.

Some people smoke not for the pleasure but for the pain. It's a symbolic way of acknowledging to yourself and others that your life isn't quite right, that you've done wrong and deserve to be punished. For some, the ashes are an external representation of the dirt that they feel is inside—an expression of self-hate.

She Ate The Whole Thing

Who among us hasn't, at one time or another, run amuck and eaten most or all of a chocolate cream pie? Or single-handedly polished off a bag of cookies, a pizza or a carton of ice cream?

Who among us hasn't raided the candy from a child's Easter basket or Halloween trick-or-treat bag? Or made a dinner of three quarter-pounders with cheese and a large order of french fries? I hope some of you haven't.

There are many people who spend their nights going from convenience store to convenience store, junk-food restaurant to junk-food restaurant, seeking relief in the consuming passion of overeating.

How often we do this may spell the difference between the person who ties one on every New Year's Eve and the alcoholic, for whom every night is New Year's Eve, or the difference between an occasional food craving and food addiction. There are theories about the chemical reward systems involved: some talk about serotonin, others about cholecystinin. But whatever the specifics, eating food is naturally very rewarding.

Chocolate is one of my drugs of choice. Eating it stimulates the body's release of phenylethyl-amine, which is similar to amphetamines. Chocolate is referred to as the "love drug" by Michael Leibowitz in The *Chemistry of Love* because of its effects on the brain's reward system. That's why we give chocolate on Valentine's Day; it's a potent releaser of several different reward chemicals.

In addition to chocolate, compulsive overeaters turn to carbohydrates—sugar, white bread, crackers, pasta, and a wide range of other "comfort foods."

We speak metaphorically of lovesick individuals turning to other substances and behaviors to fill them up; in the case of lovesick food addicts it is not a metaphor. They are, as Jeanine Roth said in her book by the same title, feeding the hungry heart. The feeding, however, is not related to any need for calories, but is related instead to a need to fill an emptiness inside and soothe a sense of not being loved or lovable.

Of course, the unbroken cycle is that the more people eat, the more they hate themselves. The heavier they become, the less lovable they feel; the less love they get, the more they eat.

Sadly, the next stop for desperate overeaters is signing up for one of many quick weight loss programs. There are at least two problems with this course: First, the weight lost will include both muscle and fat. Since calories are burned in the muscles, when muscle tissue is lost, so is the ability to burn calories in the future. Ironically, a quick weight-loss program often results in a person having a higher fat-to-muscle ratio than when they began the diet. To further complicate matters, the body adapts to a reduced-calorie diet by going into "starvation mode"—the metabolic rate drops dramatically and thus, the body can function on fewer calories than before. This evolutionary adaption meant that humans could survive during periods of famine. What this means for today's dieter is that it takes fewer calories to gain more weight. The more they lose, the more they regain.

The other problem, of course, is that the quick weight loss does not change the way compulsive overeaters feel about themselves—fat or thin. The food was addressing an emotional neediness which thinness, a new boyfriend or even popularity will never, ever satisfy. It goes deeper than the commercial suggests.

A Slow Death

It may be possible for someone to overdose on chocolate, and on rare occasions, a person may be rushed to an emergency room from an eating binge. But these are extreme consequences which most compulsive overeaters never experience. In the long-term, however, this compulsive behavior puts thousands of people in hospital beds with overeating-related conditions. Heart disease, falls and diabetes are the best-known health problems associated with compulsive overeating. Many, many more food addicts are imprisoned within their bodies and their homes; unlike heroin addicts, food addicts are not sent to prison—they carry their prisons around with them.

A large number of people, perhaps 50 to 60 million Americans, fall into the category of compulsive overeaters. Then there's a subset who binge and then purge. They throw up partly as a way of managing their weight and partly as a way of punishing themselves or attempting to gain some control over their bodies and over their parents. Purging produces damage to the teeth and the body, not to mention the toll it takes on self-esteem and the way it increases unmanageability—all for love.

Addicted To Sex

Some non-substance addictions have a biological basis to them, an obvious linkage with certain brain chemical systems—like sex. Sexual addiction is very common, but only in the past few years has it has come out of the closet. Patrick Carnes helped to bring it out with a book called *Out of the Shadows.* Although Kraft-Ebbing, a contemporary of Freud, had identified individuals who exhibited sexual compulsions, it wasn't until Carnes that sexual addiction was identified as such.

What does it mean to be addicted to sex? Most people enjoy sex and get great pleasure from it, but that does not make a person a sex addict. Sex addicts feel compelled to engage in sexual behavior even though it puts their well-being at risk. Some examples: illicit affairs which end a marriage, sexual harrassment on the job, child molestation, rape, compulsive masturbation (masturbating consecutively seven, eight, nine times—to the point of numbness or injury), going to prostitutes and risking exposure to AIDS, and other acts that invariably risk humiliation or legal consequences. These are the symptoms of sex addiction.

The power of sexual addiction comes from activating our basic reward systems, just like alcohol and drug addiction do. The sex addict, however, isn't getting much pleasure. The brief, fleeting pleasure of orgasm is quickly followed by shame, self-hate and disgust. As Carnes describes it, at the core of the sex addict's identity is a sense of being unlovable and unworthy, and sex is a way of eliminating those feelings. Their compulsive sex acts are a way of blotting out these feelings and escaping from themselves.

The French call an orgasm *la petite morte*—the small death. That's exactly what sex addicts are aiming for: death of the self, or oblivion.

This helps to explain sex addicts' ritualistic behavior. They follow certain patterns of behavior and go into a trancelike state where they lose themselves prior to, during and after the sex act. It's a type of a fugue or what alcoholics call blackouts.

How frequently these addicts engage in their sexual choice is not particularly relevant from a diagnostic standpoint. The issue is whether the sexual behavior is creating serious problems.

Sex addiction has progressive characteristics, much like alcoholism and other addictions. For instance, Carnes says that when addicts are committing crimes and engaging in potentially life-threatening and freedom-threatening activity, such as the rapist or child molester, they are at the "advanced" level. People who repeatedly rent videos and masturbate a half dozen times a day are suffering from isolation and not developing relationships, but they are not hurting anyone yet. Just as alcoholics must continually increase the dose, sex addicts may also go from one level of their addiction to the next. Pornography or other stimuli aren't what make a sex addict, just as alcohol doesn't make the alcoholic. Not surprisingly, Carnes reports that most of the sexual addicts he has treated were sexually abused as children. This abuse leads to feelings of unworthiness and shame. They see themselves as violated and thus unworthy of finding the love they so desperately want. To silence their need, they turn to the very acts that created their shame.

Alcohol: How To Win Friends And Influence Brain Cells

Everything that's been said about nicotine—the desire to look cool, to look grown-up, to be solid with the in-crowd—applies equally to alcohol. Short-term, alcohol is effective at wiping out feelings of isolation, loneliness and inadequacy. People who are fearful of others, but desperately in need of friendship and love, can connect with others through drinking. It creates an illusion of intimacy.

Alcohol relieves the sense of being awkward, ugly, unlovable. For teenagers, it increases their status while blotting out feelings of pain and fear of rejection. Alcohol does so much for so little, thus its popularity.

Alcohol is another of our legal, socially sanctioned addictions. It is potent in terms of achieving the user's initial desires, and is also toxic, causing incredible unmanageability in terms of hospitalizations, injuries, fire deaths, domestic disputes, abuse of children, car accidents, liver disease, heart disease, cancer, broken families, problems on the job. Impressive, isn't it, in a hell and damnation sort of way?

People can, and thousands do every year, drink themselves to death. Perfectly intelligent people, brilliant people, keep drinking despite mounting personal problems and loss.

Why do people continue to use alcohol after it begins to destroy them? As mentioned earlier, as a result of repeated high doses of alcohol the chemistry of the brain has been changed in ways that are often genetically predetermined. Once sufficient amounts of alcohol have been poured into their bodies and brains, the alcoholics' reward systems go awry. The brain "thinks" it must have alcohol to function.

To get the brain to rethink this issue, it must be retrained. Six months or even six years after their last drink, alcoholics still have a steady state of emptiness and neediness, unless a healthy recovery program has been initiated.

All alcoholics can say that at one time alcohol was doing wonderful things for them. For one thing, it was covering up uncomfortable emotions. When they quit drinking, they lost that protection. There was no internal personal capacity to cope with those deficits, those painful emotions. So the allure of alcohol increases each day that alcoholics stay sober unless they find other ways of filling the void.

The ultimate irony is that people who turn to alcohol to banish isolation wind up even more isolated. Not wanting others to see the amount and the effects of their imbibing, they do their drinking alone. The myth of the jolly camaraderie of the taproom is just that—a myth.

The amount of alcohol consumed isn't necessarily an indication of whether people have an addiction. Some people drink large amounts frequently and regularly without becoming alcoholics. On the other hand, some very severe alcoholics may go weeks or even months without having a drop but eventually will hear and obey the siren's call to return to that which is killing them.

That call to return to drinking is usually preceded by threats of loss or actual loss of love. Love loss is unbearable to alcoholics. It is also predictable, given the usual effects of alcohol. Confronted with a potentially loveless life, alcoholics say "to hell with it" and dive right back in.

Universal Eye-Opener

Next up is caffeine. I am a little uncomfortable in that I have a cup of coffee sitting by me at this very moment. So let me begin by *quickly* stating that caffeine is a relatively safe substance. Nevertheless, it does have a legion of low-grade addicts lining up daily, cups in hand.

Caffeine is a stimulant that produces a mild euphoria. It is well known that millions of Americans cannot start their day without one or more cups of java. If deprived of their brew, an array of withdrawal symptoms including agitation, depression, lethargy, headaches and anxiety kick in. I worked with a secretary once who turned almost homicidal when our company switched to decaf without telling her. She was shaking and in a rage as we drove out to the convenience store to get her dose.

In the general scheme of things, caffeine is a relatively benign chemical, though it clearly has addictive properties. Caffeine may have a number of benefits. Voltaire reported that he drank 20 cups of coffee a day and did his best writing under the influence of caffeine. Under the influence, old Voltaire also insulted a few people and ended up in prison a couple of times for the things he said. We might attribute that to being either too witty or "over-amped."

I don't see the connection between caffeine and lovesickness, actually. So forget it and drink up.—*A message brought to you by the World Coffee Council!*

Sleep It Off

Sleep is a wonderful way of escaping from yourself, particularly if you use sleeping pills, barbiturates or alcohol to fall asleep. With sleep you can escape from yourself for hours. Going unconscious as nature intended is a safe, nontoxic way to deal with lovesickness.

Some people spend their lives working and sleeping, and do very little in between. They go to work, they pay their bills, they don't bother anybody and they don't hurt anybody. They just sleep alot.

To the outside world, they're harmless, so the stigma associated with this addiction is zero. Family members or friends may think they're odd and may feel cheated by being deprived of the sleeper's presence. But they can't do much obvious harm with the covers pulled up over their heads.

Some people who sleep a lot may be suffering from clinical depression. "Normal" depression is a symptom of lovesickness, but there are biological depressions that have as one of their symptoms *hyper-sleep*, which has nothing to do with lovesickness. Other medical conditions, too, may leave a person exhausted and needing many hours of sleep. That's different from the experience of sleep addicts, who are using sleep as way of dealing with their sense of unlovableness and unworthiness.

Lost In Work

Just as you can lose yourself in sleep, you can lose yourself in work. Workaholics throw themselves into a whirlwind of activity to escape from themselves and their sense of inadequacy.

There are 168 hours in a week, and the work addict tries to work as many of them as possible. Work addicts may not be all that productive, and they may be running in circles, but they look busy. There's a saying: The good news is we're going a thousand miles an hour; the bad news is we're lost.

Some work addicts are not lost and, in fact are very productive. They combine work addiction with approval addiction and status addiction (addiction to possessions and power). All these get rolled up together and it feels real good for quite a while. Make them take a vacation and these people bring a laptop computer with them. Their family life suffers, of course. The families, at best, learn to live without the work addict, consoling themselves with the money and privileges that his or her efforts produce.

The personal life of work addicts may be very limited and vacuous. They have a wide array of associates but no one they really think of as a close friend. They have accomplished many things but few that really give them a sense of fulfillment or joy. Work addicts are trapped by work addiction because everyone around them is rooting for them and cheering them on (particularly if the addict is the boss). Typically, work addicts believe many people depend on them to work as hard as they do. This is as close as they get to intimacy.

Work addicts usually don't have a clue why they're working 70 hours a week. Many have a heart attack at an early age. Their contact with the life force is minimal, so they check out early.

Once again, it's not working hard in and of itself that is the addiction, just as drinking alcohol isn't alcoholism. It's the degree to which people feel compelled to work in order to avoid themselves, their angst, their lovesickness.

Putting It On The Line

Gambling addicts stimulate their reward systems by playing a never-ending game of You Bet Your Life. Robert Custard, who's done pioneering research on compulsive gambling, found that in the early history of typical compulsive gamblers, there was a time during childhood or the teenage years when they made as much money on one roll of the dice or one hand of cards as they normally would have made in an entire year. That experience has to be incredibly rewarding and causes a tremendous release of reward chemicals in the brain. The compulsive gambler is then forever in pursuit of that pot of gold.

The dilemma for gamblers is that *losing* at roulette or cards or in the stock market also produces a chemical reaction within their brain which tends to compel them to stick to it and chase the bet with another.

The gambling addict lives in a constant state of agitation. The compulsive gambler refers to this as the action. Their whole consciousness is wrapped up in the action, the game, the play, the money, the angles, the what-ifs.

The casinos or other gambling institutions play off the compulsive gambler's need to be the big shot. Many compulsive gamblers flaunt their wealth as a way of propping themselves up. They are egomaniacs with inferiority complexes. The bigger the act, the more inferior and inadequate they feel inside. Their way of dealing with their sense of inadequacy is to have money, be the high roller, be the big winner or the big loser. Of course the gambling institutions manipulate the compulsive gambler by treating him like a VIP. For stroking his ego and allowing him to play the big wheel, he'll give the gambling institutions all his money.

The higher the stakes, the bigger the buzz. Just as the alcoholic is not really interested in drinking just one beer, the compulsive gambler needs to place progressively higher bets in order to achieve his trancelike experience. Gambling is often intensely painful for the compulsive gambler, win, lose or draw, but especially if he loses.

We see this on Wall Street as well; for many it's the ideal arena for compulsive gambling. There are dozens of ways to risk your money—stocks, bonds, options, puts, calls, buying on margin.

Like work addicts, brilliant gamblers can make a million dollars and still feel miserable. The criterion is not whether gamblers end up leaving with more money than when they started; it's the internal experience—does it satisfy, does it fulfill? Does the three-carat diamond pinky ring make them feel good inside or are they still a loser down inside? Do they live a life of desperation punctuated by the occasional jackpot?

Like our other addicts, compulsive gamblers are attempting to fill their emptiness; they do it with plastic chips and phone calls from their stockbroker or bookie.

Slaves Of Sweat

Studies have shown that intense exercise for 40 minutes or more will produce the release of dopamine, endorphins and probably other brain reward chemicals. Physical fitness addicts use exercise as a way of stimulating those reward systems, hoping to gain a sense of being more lovable and more worthy of love.

Exercising takes up time, filling the waking hours of people who are chronically lonely or bored. If pursued long enough, they feel better and look better. At the same time, they achieve a sense of belonging because they're working out at the gym or running with others, and even though there may be little interaction with these companions, there's an illusion of connectedness.

By becoming more attractive, exercise addicts believe they will find the love they need. This illusion is one that's well reinforced in our media—a beautiful body attracts love.The problem is that only the body gets the love. The love lands on their body, not them. Lose the gorgeous body and you're likely to lose the love. Consequently, like a muscle-bound hamster on a running wheel, exercise addicts run away from their greatest fear—being less than beautiful and hence unloved.

A close relative of exercise addiction is bodybuilding addiction. It often involves the use of illegal steroids to create large muscle mass and muscle definition. This phenomenon adds achievement addiction and status addiction to exercise addiction. The larger and more powerful the bodybuilding addict gets, the more approval and love they think they'll get. Needless to say, bodybuilding takes a great deal of time, and hours of curls and bench presses are a great escape (all addicts are escape artists). With their newly developed armor, they are sure the arrows of rejection and ridicule can be avoided.

Exercise in and of itself is great activity. Exercise is good for you. If carried to extremes, it becomes a consuming passion but not one that is stigmatized. Not in the least. But anything pushed to the extreme can be harmful. You can get torn ligaments and shin splints; you can have a heart attack or get hit by a car while jogging. The use of steroids can cause physical and psychological problems, ranging from rage to impotence to cancer.

You've crossed the line from constructive exercising to addictive exercising if you continue doing so even if it is becoming destructive to your body and your social life.

Addicts often get up in the middle of the night to exercise, and insist on working out even if they are sick. They feel guilty and anxious if they haven't done their 10-mile run. Exercise extremists, like the rest of our addicts, aren't running in pursuit of something; they're running away from something.

In Love With Love

Love addicts think they're pursuing the real thing. Who can be against love? What love addicts are seeking, though, is the perfect relationship. The lover who will *love* them, *care for* them and *never leave* them. Fair enough. These are reasonable desires. The only problem is, love addicts don't love themselves. They are forever trying to escape from themselves by running into the arms of another.

Everything that was previously said about the adolescent love affair applies to love addicts. In that sense, love addicts are the purest example of lovesickness, because they are attempting to satisfy lovesickness through a love relationship. They don't realize that it is impossible to satisfy lovesickness through a relationship with just one individual because one individual can't love you unconditionally, and this is what the love addict wants more than anything.

Because love addicts persist in the mistaken belief that if they find the *right* person their life will be okay, they keep going from one relationship to another. Each time, they experience the whole process of euphoria to tolerance to withdrawal, sometimes very rapidly. On occasion love addicts have an entire relationship without the other person knowing it, because the relationship played itself out in the love addict's mind. Some people act out their love addiction vicariously, through soap operas, television dramas or Gothic romance novels. (Gothic romances are the best-selling fiction books because so many are bought and read compulsively by relationship/love addicts.)

As with all lovesick individuals, love addicts have no love for themselves; they feel unworthy of being loved. Like Groucho Marx, who said he'd never want to belong to a club that would have him as a member, love addicts shy away from a relationship with anyone who would accept them. The psycho-logic goes like this: "I'm a worthless phony devoid of any real quality. If 'Joe' loves me, then he must be a loser, too. Therefore, I'm no longer interested in him."

When love addicts get involved with someone who rejects them, on the other hand, they'll continue to pursue, becoming fixated on that person. In this case, the internal psychological dynamic goes something like this: "The person who rejects me knows what's going on, they can see that I'm not lovable. They know the truth about me. That's the person I want." In addition, because of their poor self-image, love addicts tend to believe they deserve to suffer and be rejected. It hurts so good. They are playing out a script in which rejection and abandonment confirm deeply felt beliefs about themselves and what they deserve.

Love addicts never get the love they need, because they're always either rejecting someone who would be good for them or pursuing someone who is bound to reject them.

In the late 1970s and 1980s, the concept of co-dependence was very much in vogue. But the book that popularized the concept included eight pages of symptoms—the signs and the characteristics of the co-dependent person. This alone suggests that the net was cast too far, that the concept was too vague and fuzzy and all-encompassing; everyone qualified as co-dependent.

The criteria for love addiction is simple: if people keep getting involved in relationships that make their life a mess, then they are love addicted. The bigger the mess, the worse the addiction. The more needy I am, the more likely I am to repeatedly get into relationships that are going to be harmful to me.

On occasions when a love addict gets involved with someone who is capable of a healthy relationship, one of two things tend to occur: Either the healthy individual will try to help the lovesick individual to become healthy or the healthier individual will walk away. A healthy individual does not want to stay in a relationship with someone who is lovesick for very long because the healthy individual begins to experience the lovesick partner as a vacuum. The bigger the vacuum, the more the relationship will suck.

Money And Power

I have lumped "money, status, possessions and power" addictions together because they are all basically interchangeable. If I have money, I have power; if I have power, I get money and so on. It all boils down to finding ways of propping up an inadequate sense of self with this, that and the other thing.

Money, power, prestige and nice stuff are great if used constructively in a healthy, loving fashion. The lovesick power/money addict uses *people* and loves *things*. It should be the other way around.

Power is an effective aphrodisiac. Ditto with money and status. The power addict goes about working angles and deals to accrue more of this influential drug, not for the good it might do others, but because he is driven to do so. Society stands in awe of such individuals, thus confirming to them that they are on the right track. So why do so many of them report that they feel hollow?

The problem, of course, is that the affection they receive from others never seems genuine. In the back of their minds is always the thought that they are "loved" because of their possessions, power and prestige. And they are often right.

In the hot pursuit of their drug, they have left some carnage along the trail. Damaged relations don't disappear. A remnant of each is left rotting inside each power addict. Each lie and each "screw you" takes a small part of the addict's own life away. If they treat others this way, how can they expect to be treated? They either feel that they've been fooling everyone or that their partner, friends, family and business associates are the ones who are being phony, manipulative and scheming. So they're always distrustful of the affection they're being given. They seldom if ever experience a sense of peace, satisfaction and serenity.

Money and power are perhaps the most seductive addictions around. Few are chosen and fewer still get to indulge in the really high-test stuff. Even those who have always had money and power often have a hard time managing it. It's just too intoxicating. To handle strong doses of power or money, one must have equally strong doses of unconditional love—the one thing that money can never buy.

They Shop Till They Drop

Shopping addiction could be a subset of the money and power addiction except that people who have very little money or power have gotten caught up in it. Shopping addicts get their high from buying things, of course. Some buy to give things away because in doing so they think they can cement their relationships and assure themselves of love.

Some shopping addicts accumulate unnecessary things as a way of filling themselves up, of giving themselves psychic boosts and a false sense of security. Interaction at the store, being treated pleasantly by the sales clerks, displaying a credit card that demonstrates their affluence and walking off with the valuable package—all this makes them feel important.

Shopping brings on a dizzying feeling of euphoria for the addict: buzzing around the store, filling the shopping cart, arms full of purchases. These are illusions of power, purpose and importance. One compulsive shopper I worked with would buy dozens of the same thing and never wear any of them. For instance, she'd buy the same blouse in different colors but never wear any of them. But by cluttering her closets with all these possessions, she had made her world more substantial and herself more lovable. Or so she thought.

For some shopping addicts, shopping becomes a way of punishing themselves. By spending beyond their means and going deeper into debt, they hammer away at themselves, abusing themselves economically. Some destroy their credit rating as a way to control their compulsive spending. If they don't have credit, they think they can't get into too much trouble. Unfortunately, their delusion keeps them from seeing that they are *already* in trouble.

Lovesickness is never satisfied with things; inner emptiness returns as the shopping bags are emptied.

Rage-aholics

For several years I worked in a prison with alcohol- and drug-addicted inmates. Without exception, the addicts were people who were desperately hungry for acceptance and belonging. Many felt such an extreme hunger that they did not dare to attempt to fulfill it. In attempting to find love and acceptance, they risked further rejection. So instead they learned to build a thick skin of hate and anger and meanness.

Hate is a tried and true defense. As the saying goes, the best defense is offense, and those who get caught in the world of illegal drugs and crime are veterans of offensiveness. The pain of these addicts is old and impacted. Rage stuffed from childhood hardens and gets jagged. I have seen many of these angry, raging souls find peace but the recovery process for them is long and requires tremendous determination.

And Other Shackles

When addiction is mentioned, people tend to think of heroin and cocaine and other illegal drugs. All that has been written about drug addiction applies equally to prescription drugs and over-the-counter drugs when they, too, are abused. The substance is not important. For the addict, the act of taking drugs is an attempt to medicate an internal sense of lovelessness and unworthiness.

PART TWO

The Lovesickness Cure

CHAPTER 4

Reliable Sources Of Unconditional Love

The Good Stuff

Now that we have an idea what lovesickness is, what causes it and how it is manifested, what can we do about it? Periodically I've referred to "reliable sources of unconditional love" as the good stuff, the stuff that feeds our soul and heals our lovesickness. Now let's take a close look at what does and does not qualify as a reliable source of unconditional love.

First of all, for something to be a "reliable source," it must always be at least potentially available every single day. Regardless of where we are or what time it is, for it to be reliable it's always got to be on tap.

"Unconditional" means that there are no strings attached. There's no tradeoff. It's freely given without any expectation that the giver will get something back. It's there for the asking; it's even available without asking.

And unlike romantic, frantic love, we are interested in the kind of love that is characterized by a strong interest in someone's well-being; that gives attention, affection, direction, concern and care; that seeks to care for, comfort and assist.

Unconditional love is quite different from infatuation or the adolescent love described in Chapter 1. Infatuation is like cotton candy—tasty perhaps, but you better not try to live on it. Unconditional love is more like our fruits and veggies—healthful and life sustaining. Compared to cotton candy it's less sensational and colorful, but it gives us serenity and depth instead. In time, we can develop a taste for it.

Unconditional love feeds the soul. It is the stuff from which emotional security and peace of mind are made.

There are *three and one-half* reliable sources of unconditional love. They only exist, however, as "potential sources" because each has one or more obstacles associated with obtaining it. Many people are unwilling to go to the effort necessary to make these sources a part of their lives. Some people insist on holding onto beliefs that interfere with accessing one or more of these sources of unconditional love. Still, at least one of these sources is ready-made for you, and available now with little stress or strain.

The three and one-half reliable sources of unconditional love are: God, self, a loving community and pets. Pets are the one-half.

You'll notice that the list does not include another person. Lovesick people desperately believe that there's a special someone out there who will love them so totally that all their neediness and loneliness and emptiness will disappear. I've never seen it happen, at least not for more than a few months. Ultimately, the euphoria wears thin and the conditionality of the love comes through.

The Ultimate Source

For the God-phobic among us, I'd like to offer a few assurances: First, the approach taken here is nondenominational and as universal as possible, drawing from various spiritual traditions. Borrowing from Alcoholics Anonymous, we will talk in terms of a "power greater than ourselves" rather than of an old man with a bad temper. Second, I promise not to preach. I've shown this to a couple of my hardcore atheist friends and they have given it a low rating on their "bull meter." One even liked it. Finally, if you are among the many who have been betrayed, mistreated or simply bored by spiritual mumbo jumbo, I promise to be brief.

The simple fact is that there are millions of people who have found great strength, support and comfort from the development of a spiritual orientation. Many others have a poorly developed image of God: they believe in something, but they get stuck when pressed to describe those beliefs.

For many people, there is difficulty in accessing God. Perhaps they were raised in a religious tradition whose God is vengeful, threatening and angry. "I don't need a God," these people say, "if He's going to be condemning me or on vacation."

We all know of people who seem to have a relationship with God that serves as a source of strength, joy and peace. At least in part because of their spiritual beliefs people have been able to withstand all kinds of deprivation.

This God of joy and peace is a potential source of unconditional love because He (or She) can be loving and available to us until the day we die—indeed, beyond death.

In speaking of God, I mean a natural force of the universe and beyond, a spiritual and divine force that is available to us all the time and provides love, direction, support, comfort and the power to do things, provided those things are in harmony with His will.

Recognizing that some people do not or cannot believe in God, 12-Step fellowships speak of a Higher Power, which encompasses any entity or force or concept that's bigger than ourselves, without all of the baggage that our religious education or prior religious experiences may have instilled. I will talk further about this, but in the meantime keep your mind open when you read Chapter 5.

Look Within

The second potential source of unconditional love is one's self.

I'm going to be with me until the day I die. I have no idea what happens after that point but, clearly, I'm with me for life. Moreover, I can be a source of love for myself. I can learn to love myself unconditionally.

Many people have been trained from childhood to despise themselves. Some like themselves only if they do well; the rest of the time they have a neutral or poor opinion of themselves. Their self-esteem is dependent upon how close they come to measuring up to their own standards or the standards that have been taught to them by their parents and by society. This is *conditional* love. Conditional love can feel nice, but it is essentially just a type of manipulation. "If I'm a good boy, then I get a gold star." It's very different from getting a gold star simply because you're worthy and lovable and deserving of the best.

Many people fear that if they were to love themselves unconditionally they would turn into horrid, egotistical, self-centered human beings.

Contrary to appearances, egotistical and narcissistic people actually despise themselves. They have very little self-love. Their acts of self-adulation and mirror gazing are driven by a very fragile and insecure sense of self. They feel so poorly about themselves that they must forever work the audience for applause. They pose, posture and praise themselves because they're deathly afraid that no one else will. And they need that approval so very badly. Sadly, they may even be partly aware that they push people away with their bragging and prancing. But they can't help it. They, too, you see, are lovesick. Their efforts at commanding attention and approval is desperate because of the emptiness they feel.

People with unconditional self-love are right-sized, secure and at ease with themselves and others. They're not working the crowd for approval because they have enough of their own. They know their worth and are comfortable in this knowledge.

Those who have sufficient unconditional love for themselves are able to take a stand for that which is unpopular and withstand the censure of the crowd. Such people have been the true leaders and visionaries of our time.

Falling in love with yourself is not easy. How do you do it

in a healthy, appropriate way? What are the steps that get you from self-hate to self-love? What are the points of transition? We'll answer those questions and others in Chapters 6 and 7.

Group Love

In Chapter 8, we'll look in depth at loving communities or fellowships as sources of unconditional love. Except for ourselves, no other *individual* can ever fulfill the role of providing a reliable source of unconditional love. We need to have a community of other people available in the form of a living, organic community that has as its basic, core value or ethic the unconditional acceptance and love of its members.

Where do we find these kinds of groups? Probably the best-known source in our society today is the 12-Step fellowships such as Alcoholics Anonymous, Narcotics Anonymous, Overeaters Anonymous, Smokers Anonymous and various other groups formed to meet specific needs. Other support groups, with or without 12 Steps, are springing up all around because of the needs they are filling.

Our families, too, can become a potential source of unconditional love; so can civic and religious groups. Within such groups there may be camaraderie and a sense of community, and some may achieve the levels of intimacy and unconditionality of which we've been speaking. Even those groups which fall far short of our ideal offer a starting point.

Groups that have as their stated value unconditional love and whose traditions and guidelines encourage this loving ethic are the hardest to find. It's difficult for many people to become part of such a group. How do you join a 12-Step fellowship, assuming you qualify for membership? How do you transform your own family or create a family that has unconditional love as its core value? These are among the points that will be addressed in Chapter 8.

Calling Doctor Spot!

Finally, our last reliable source of unconditional love, the one-half that was referred to earlier: pets.

Critics among us, particularly those who have never

owned a pet, may quarrel over whether pets actually love us. Indeed, a strong argument can be made that pets are not capable of true love, that they are only capable of expressing their need for us, and that this only feels like love to us. Well, I don't know. For the person who has a loving critter sitting by her side or on her lap, there is no argument. Certain pets—most dogs and some cats—have the capacity to never have a bad day and always be there for their human friend.

The wagging tail, the purring, the rubbing up against the leg, the cuddling at night, the eye contact and the nuzzling—animal-human interaction somehow releases within the human being a feeling of true love that for many people surpasses anything ever experienced with another person. The fact that animals are able to do this on a consistent basis enables them to qualify as reliable source of unconditional love. They don't meet the full standard, and are only one-half, because, sad to say, they are more likely to die before their human partner. The good news, though, is you can always go to the animal shelter, rescue another and develop a new loving relationship.

In Chapter 9—the dessert of this book—I'll expand on this concept and outline some guidelines for selecting a loving pet.

There are a few general points worth making about unconditional love and where it can and can't be found.

Counterfeit Love

That Special Someone

The single most common error people make is attempting to get the love they need from *one* other human being. That special somebody. The backlog in divorce courts and domestic abuse centers is compelling evidence that Cupid ought to either get his arrows or his glasses checked. Or better yet, both. Romantic affairs are great fun, but nothing to stake your emotional stability on. Infatuation is the basis for much craziness and turmoil, but it's not salvation.

Even after things have settled down, and the young lovers are older and wiser, there is no use expecting your lover to serve as the fount from whom all of one's love needs will be fulfilled. One obvious problem is that, like a pet, spouses and lovers die. Unlike pets, however, good ones are harder to come by. Mortality aside, when we expect one person to fulfill our emotional neediness, what happens when he or she has a bad day, a headache, an affair, gets lost driving home or just doesn't come home? If all your emotional eggs are in one basket, what happens if the other person changes his mind? It has been reported that among older couples when one dies the other is likely to die in the following year.

While this notion of marital symbiosis sounds nice and gushy, the reality is actually rather sad for the partner who is left behind and dies of a broken heart. Why not diversify one's dependency?

And now that we're on the subject, how many individuals are actually capable of loving unconditionally? Whether it's a marriage relationship or some other coupling, each person typically has a list of unspoken conditions he or she expects to have met. If both partners are psychic and competent at mind reading, this is fine. In the healthier relationships, however, these conditions are articulated and renegotiated periodically. In either case, conditions do exist! Lots of them.

The old saying that men are looking for "sex objects" and women are looking for "success objects" may be shallow but it does summarize two of the more common conditions that exist in relationships. There are long lists of conditions why people come together and that's all fine. Good conditional relationships between two people are wonderful, and the world depends on them, but they're not to be mistaken for unconditional love. They will not, by themselves, sustain us.

The idea which has been foisted upon most of us by our parents and the popular media is that if you've found the right one, your emotional needs will be securely handled till death do you part. Let's look at the numbers.

About half all of marriages end in divorce. Of those that don't divorce, many stay together because of economic necessity or the children. What's that leave? Maybe 20 or 25 percent of folks who are staying together by choice. Here we have our bride and groom pledging holy oaths and sweet somethings before family and God—to love, honor and respect one another forever. Four years later, their lawyers are discussing settlement arrangements on the golf course.

Gosh, I sound down on marriage, don't I? Sorry about that. My point is simply that married people will do much better and single people will do much better if they don't look to one human being for all their love.

The Kids

People also look for unconditional love from their children. Ho, ho, ho! Many a parent gets suckered into believing that this little baby who's staring up and saying "goo-goo" and "ah-ah" will be eternally grateful for the gift of life.

This notion gets blown to bits when baby turns two years old and learns how to say "No." If anything, the child is unconditionally frustrating. It's not the child's job to be unconditionally loving. On the contrary, it's the parent's job to give unconditional love to that child. And that's tough work for most of us.

To truly love someone unconditionally requires tremendous personal development. Essentially, to be able to love another unconditionally, you have to have unconditional love for yourself—enough so that you have extra to give away. Only individuals who have done the work to develop reliable sources of unconditional love are able to give it freely; in fact, it's the only thing you can do with love: pass it on.

If you *need* someone, you can't love him or her unconditionally. To be a good parent, you can't need your child's love. If a parent needs a child's attention, acceptance or approval, that parent is going to make decisions based upon the child's desires, not on prudence. The parent is seeking the child's approval.

Lovesick parents are blinded by their own neediness; they turn to their children for love and confuse their dependency with love. But their children are expressing *need*, not love. In time, as the children's own neediness matures into addictive and destructive behaviors, both the parent and child are heartbroken and resentful. Both were looking to the other for love and got only neediness instead.

A colleague and I once printed a parent/child greeting card that said on the front cover, "No! No! No! No! No! No!" in white letters against a stark, black background. When the card was opened, there was a big red heart with the words: "To NO you is to love you."

The parent who loves a child unconditionally is the parent who is able to take a stand that's in the child's best interest, with little concern for whether the decision is going to damage the child's affection for the parent. The all-loving parent is concerned about the child's well-being unconditionally, even if the child disagrees.

I have worked with families where parents were so lovesick that they turned to their own children for affection and acceptance. In several cases, sexual abuse of one kind or another had occurred. Even when this was not the case, the child's development was invariably warped by the parents' dependence upon them for "love." In most of these cases there was a "spousification" of the child by a single parent (or a parent whose real spouse was emotionally unavailable). The child was expected to fulfill the parent's neediness. In these situations, the parent/child relationship is upside-down.

When parents substitute permissiveness and indulgence for caring discipline and responsible guidance, they are trying to get the child to feed them emotionally.

The needier the parent, the more likely he or she is to fall into this trap. And it is a trap. The lovesick parent is just as desperate for love as a heroin addict; in both cases their child's welfare is put at risk because of misguided efforts at reducing lovesickness.

As the indulged child of a lovesick parent grows older, he or she is likely to become the opposite of what the parent expected. Rather than being grateful and loving, the child is a resentful, angry terrorist. Why? Because the child was ripped off by the parent and received *need* instead of love.

Overlapping Love Sources

There's a strong connection between each of the reliable sources of unconditional love. One eventually leads to others. For example, once you begin to love yourself unconditionally, you are likely to begin seeing a spiritual dimension to life. You begin to recognize the divinity within and without. You also begin to develop a sense of oneness, a sense of community with other people. Those who have developed an abundance of healthy self-love will also tend to take pleasure in the fellowship of life and nature in all of its forms, including pets.

For some reason which I haven't yet figured out, a love relationship with your poodle is somewhat less likely to lead to a love relationship with yourself, God or others. This is partly why pets are only half a reliable source of unconditional love. Starting with any of the three sources, however, will eventually lead you to others.

Beginning With God

If you first experience yourself as being loved by God, you eventually have to come to the conclusion that, if God—the Supreme Source and Infinite—loves you, who the heck are you not to love yourself? Once you settle into the idea that God loves you, you would have to have standards higher than God's to condemn yourself. And that's awfully arrogant!

Once you develop a healthy, loving relationship with a Higher Power, eventually you just have to learn to love yourself. Since you surely can't be the only one that God loves, inevitably there comes the realization that you're a fellow among fellows, one of the species who are all God's children, and that we're here to love each other. That love of others and love of God and love of pets—yes, love of pets—are all aspects of the same expression of love.

Members of 12-Step fellowships speak about how, having had a spiritual awakening, they seek to carry the message of recovery to others and to do it freely. They give it away unconditionally.

Beginning With A Loving Community

For many people, starting the search for unconditional love by seeking to attain fellowship with others is the hardest route. The sense of inadequacy that fills the lovesick person is accompanied by a strong fear of rejection. Often the lovesick person has had a history of rejection and abandonment, and so there's usually anxiety when attempting to become part of a group. Because so many groups function less than perfectly, and not everybody who shows up at their first meeting is immediately embraced in a warm, loving way, all the fears stemming from the schoolyard experiences of not fitting in come to the fore.

But it's actually quite easy to start with a fellowship if it's a community that has unconditional love of its members as its basic ethic. This ultimately leads to a discovery of spirituality and love of self, because if this group loves you eventually you get the idea that there's something about you that's lovable. Many A.A. members say their sponsor loved them or the group loved them until they were able to love themselves. And as you continue to receive freely given love, you notice that the people who give it the most freely are those who see themselves as a channel of God's love. Thus you get tuned into the spiritual source behind it all.

Communities that have unconditional love as their guiding principle tend to have a relationship with a loving God or Higher Power, and that love leads to another core value: to grow along spiritual lines and to deepen a relationship with God. By becoming part of such a group, then, I can learn to love myself and realize that there truly is a power greater than myself that is an abundant source of love.

CHAPTER 5

God As A Reliable Source Of Unconditional Love

Each of us has a particular image of God, if indeed we have one at all. The image we have in mind, which has been shaped by our experiences, has a lot to do with whether we can view God as a reliable source of love. Let's look at some of the more common images.

God As Cosmic Bellhop

Somewhere early in our childhood most of us get the idea that there is this supernatural, all powerful Being to whom we can pray, and if we say those prayers correctly and if we behave ourselves properly, then our prayers will be answered. "God listens to our prayers," we are told.

Like most children, I tried this idea out. I'm sure I prayed for lots of things early in my life: to stay up late, to beat up my older brother, to get that red firetruck. These prayers mostly went unanswered. I'm sure I concluded, however, that I was either praying incorrectly or that I was deemed unworthy by God because he seldom did what I asked.

When I was taken to Hebrew school, I saw it as a chance to learn how to pray correctly. I quickly discovered that I'd been doing it wrong because I had been saying my prayers in English. I needed to learn Hebrew! As it turned out, this was very hard for me because I was still having trouble learning to read English. Hebrew was way beyond me.

But this was the magical language. These were the ancient words of Abraham and Moses. This was the secret code I needed to learn.

My Hebrew School teacher was a special individual. He had survived the Holocaust of Nazi Germany. He told us stories about the Holocaust—it had been little more than a dozen years since that horrible time and he needed to talk about it. He showed us the numbers they had tattooed on his arm. He showed us a documentary about some of the concentration camps. And he told us about the atrocities he himself witnessed.

None of my classmates dared to ask the question, but certainly many of us had to be asking ourselves: "How could God allow this to happen to his chosen people?" Here was this teacher of Hebrew, and even he lost loved ones, even he was tortured and scarred for life. Either he deserved it or prayers simply didn't work because it was obvious that he knew *how* to pray.

As I grew older, I saw more instances of how ineffective prayer was in bailing people out of jams. Starving children, disease, war and tragedies of all kinds seemed to be visited upon the prayerful and prayerless with equal frequency.

There were some people in my life who seemed to get preferred treatment by this wish-granting God. My grandmother, for example, could always get the cards she wanted when we played casino. She would simply say, "Give me little casino, give me little casino," and sure enough, she usually seemed to get what she wanted. This really confused me. How could God attend to my grandmother's card game and ignore the children who had nothing to eat?

Today, this image of God seems immature and primitive.

But if God isn't a bellhop ready to carry our luggage when properly asked, what does He do? And what good is He? Is He simply in retirement or perhaps still on active duty but "utterly indifferent," as Kurt Vonnegut suggested in one of his stories: "Either God cures me of my maladies, delivers me into the arms of a true love and gets me parking spaces when I need them or He's a fraud."

There are other possibilities.

God As Cop

A second silly yet common image of God, and one that I still find myself regressing to from time to time, is God as cop. Or, perhaps, as a kind of heavenly IRS auditor—an all-knowing, all-seeing, all-powerful entity whose real purpose is to catch me whenever I've done anything wrong. Not only does He catch me (given His vast intelligence network), but he metes out punishment for each and every crime. Like his assistant, Santa Claus, "he knows if you've been bad or good, so be good for goodness sake!"

It seems pretty clear that this image of God needs some fine-tuning, too. After all, there are just too many nasty people not getting caught by God, or anyone else for that matter. Columbo, He ain't! I hate to break the news, but in case you never noticed before good often goes unrewarded and evil often has the best seats in the house and the nicest house on the beach. If God *is* a cop, He should consider some other line of work. Like maybe a crossing guard.

Just like the image of God as Bellhop, God as Cop is simply a trick of our childish unconscious mind. We *need* to believe that the bad guys get punished and so our minds (following the minds of our forefathers and foremothers) create a scheme in which damnation-worthy folks in our lives get their just desserts in some unverifiable afterlife. They go off to hell when they die or maybe they come back in their next life as a mosquito or slug or gross looking spider. "Hey Bill, is that you? You nasty little bug! Serves you right." Squish!

Folks who've had this image of God beaten into them (as many of my friends and patients have) are handcuffed with a foreboding sense that they are wrong or wicked. Others feel deeply condemned and convicted of their sinfulness. Having broken one or more of the Ten Commandments, many of these "suspects" feel damned and, at least on a subconscious level, forever doomed to serve time in the celestial lockup.

The image of God as cop is held by some fairly sophisticated folks. Some (like me) are so sophisticated that actually they deny having such beliefs. But we do. We do because they were planted into our brains when we were very young and defenseless. The image was nurtured and developed by individuals and institutions that needed to keep us in line but didn't have the resources to do it without the aid of some supernatural law enforcer. Thus God was dressed in a policeman's uniform and stationed behind our bedroom door, as well as right around the corner in the locker room, not to mention all four corners of our minds.

For many of us, then, accessing God as a reliable source of unconditional love is problematic. We tend to think that God does not love unconditionally; instead, he condemns unconditionally. He is not to be sought after; rather He is to be avoided. This image of God is getting us nowhere, but it is not easily shed. Nonetheless, with awareness and time, a healthier spiritual understanding can be developed.

God As Con Artist

Thousands of individuals have been sexually abused by clergy. Many more have been financially exploited by the words of compassionate con artists: "Send your checks to me and I'll put in a good word for you with God," or words to that effect.

For people who have been victimized in these ways, the notion of there being a God of any kind is hard to imagine. For such individuals, divine help may appear forever inaccessible.

It has been my experience that many of these victims of spiritual malpractice—even those who have been severely violated—can overcome the harm they have suffered and learn to grow along spiritual lines.

God As A Reliable Source Of Unconditional Love

I'd like to suggest an image of God that is somewhat different than those just described. It is my conviction that God is a sacred and divine force that both *obeys* and *is* the law which controls the events on earth and in the universe. These laws have been described by physics, chemistry, mathematics and biology. They have also been set forth in the writings of the great spiritual teachers. They are the laws that govern the way life works. If we learn to live in harmony with these laws—God's will for us—we will have increased moments of peace, serenity and contentment even when we're faced with life's harshest challenges.

The major religions of the world have all attempted to reveal what these laws are. Their spokesmen—Moses, Mohammed, Jesus, Buddha and so on—embodied these laws and represented perfect or near-perfect expressions of these laws. Others, too, have done so with far less notice. There is one Light but many lamps.

Similarly, the sciences are unraveling the wonders of physical matter. These, too, are God's laws. To the degree that we as individuals and as a collective species live in accordance with the discovered laws, we will experience ever greater levels of comfort, joy and peace.

A law that seems to govern human existence is the Law of Self-fulfilling Prophecy. Basically, the law states that we tend to get what we expect to get. If we expect rejection, we will get rejection. If we expect condemnation, we will get condemnation. Not always, but there will be a tendency over time for our expectations to be fulfilled. The mind tends to find opportunities to prove itself correct. There's a large body of psychological literature supporting this finding (psychology being the science of the mind and experience). No doubt your own experiences offer numerous examples of this law.

For this reason—that you nearly always get what you expect—I suggest that you embrace the notion of an unconditionally loving God.

Regardless of your actions, your past, your thoughts or your imperfections, begin developing the belief that you are loved totally and unconditionally by God.

What does it mean to be loved unconditionally by God? It doesn't mean that God will find you that parking space or cure you of cancer. It just doesn't seem to be the way God works. Everybody dies eventually. Everybody suffers loss and tragedy. And there simply are never going to be enough perfect parking spots.

Belief Pays Off

There are benefits, though, to developing a belief in an unconditionally loving God.

The first is a subtle sense of ourselves as essentially good and worthwhile—a heightened ability to experience ourselves as being loved and lovable. This is how it happens:

If we can develop a belief in God or a Higher Power that *loves us unconditionally*, then we too will have to love ourselves. If we don't, we are placing ourselves above God. We are being more judgmental than God. If God loves us, who are we to differ?

Similarly, as we develop a consciousness of being one of God's creations then we have reconcile with the implications of this idea. As a child of God, condemning ourselves becomes the same as condemning God. After all, we are made of God-stuff (didn't God create the universe and everything in it?). Every cell of our bodies—even the fat ones—is filled with the divine principle and spirit. So love it.

Many people have difficulty loving themselves either because of things they've done to other people or because of things done to them. People who've developed spiritually love themselves because of what they're made of. In addition to flesh and bones, they're aware of their spiritual essence; they know that there is something of God within them. Their spiritual essence, in and of itself, makes them worthy of their own love.

As we come to develop a belief in a loving God, we tend to believe that, despite appearances, all is well. We may come to feel we are cradled within the hands of God. Later I will describe a meditation utilizing this imagery. Remember: expectations influence experience. It's the law.

To the degree that we can make conscious contact with a loving God, we feel safe, secure and at peace. Even in the face of death, there are individuals who live their last days calm and serene. Such a consciousness is equally valuable in the world of work and in our interpersonal relations. It's helpful to have surety and gentleness instead of insecurity and anxiety. It's difficult to have faith and fear at the same time.

A second benefit of pursuing spiritual growth has been variously described as an "awakening" or "enlightenment." This is what is symbolized by the halo that surrounds images of Christ and Buddha and other spiritual figures in religious paintings. Some who have had the experience of an awakening talk about a radiance or aura that they feel. Pursuing a spiritual awakening as if it were just another high, though, doesn't get the job done. It's not something to pursue as an end in itself. On the other hand, it is something that, as an act of grace, can and does occur.

Most spiritual awakenings are spoken of in religious literature as being incredibly profound events that only occur to divine leaders, but my own research makes it clear that everyone is capable of having them, and that many have.

One morning early in my recovery, I was listening to some gospel music on the radio. Though it was from a very different religious tradition than my own, I found myself swept away into a state of spiritual ecstacy which left me weeping for joy. Spontaneously I fell to my knees and thanked God for the beauty of that moment and the intensely profound sense of being loved by God. Periodically, perhaps a half dozen times or so in my life, I've felt these moments of at-oneness with God: moments when the sense of the divine and the sense of the presence of God, oneness with God, love of God, was particularly intense.

Some people speak in terms of hearing a "voiceless voice." Others experience a *knowing* or an intuition stronger than mere intuition. Some experience a sense of being loved and directed to act in certain way, or a sense that all is well. These spiritual experiences, variously referred to as acts of grace, occur spontaneously, without any effort. People who practice prayer and meditation seem to be more inclined to have these experiences, but not on demand. There's no mystical button that can simply be pushed. But there are spiritual practices that open us to these experiences and enable us to develop a conscious contact with God.

Practice Makes Progress

For those of us who have an openness to and are comfortable with the idea of God, the instruction is really very simple. Go for it. Return to whatever religious practices make sense to you, the only caveat being to do so with the idea of developing a relationship with a *loving God.* For some, it might mean attending church or synagogue or other houses of worhsip; for others it might mean daily prayer or praying several times a day or certain other religious devotions or practices. Whatever it might be, for those who already are at ease with some religious tradition, the suggestion here is to return to and make use of that tradition.

For those who wish to grow spiritually within the framework of an organized religion, but don't have any particular religion in mind, my advice is to go shopping. Visit different religious groups. Try them out and see if any of them speak to you, fill you. You may know of people who seem to have a light in them, who seem to be buoyed and lit with spirituality. If those people are attractive to you, it's possible that their spiritual practices might be ones you'd feel comfortable with. Talk to them and try worshipping with them.

There are thousands of different religious denominations in America and around the world. New religions are also sprouting up which seem to fill a void that many of us feel. Check them out.

One word of warning about joining religious groups: As you begin your quest you may come across some organizations that are overzealous in trying to recruit you. Quite clearly there are organizations that do not exist for the welfare of their congregation but strictly for the welfare of the "spiritual" leader and hierarchy. Be wary of any group if the requests that are made of you seem excessive in terms of money, the amount of time you're to devote or the degree to which you're expected to recruit new members. Those are the three classic signs of exploitative groups which we tend to think of as a cult. These groups employ techniques to manipulate members emotionally with talk about a loving God and a charismatic leader who has a special relationship with God that members can benefit from, provided they make the proper sacrifices.

If you're seeking to build or rebuild a spiritual life and you're not comfortable belonging to *any* group or organization, or if there are none you find appealing at present, there are still many options available to you. In particular, you can begin to engage in certain spiritual practices, the most prominent of which are prayer and meditation.

Stilling The Drunken Monkey

Meditation has been used and espoused by most religious traditions and by spiritual people and mystics for thousands of years. Meditation means different things to different people. Apart from any particular religious traditions, I'll describe a few meditative practices which you might find helpful. In addition, I've identified some books that can provide additional information about meditation.

"The mind," according to Buddhist tradition, "is like a drunken monkey that's just been stung by a scorpion." Try to picture the poor chimp, jumping about from place to place, swinging by its tail, screeching, jibber-jabbering and rolling around. Does this resemble the activity of your mind? If you think not, it may be because you just haven't paid close enough attention to it.

Try this little experiment: Direct your attention to the passage of air as you breathe through your nose. Just try to keep the spotlight of your mind focused only on your breath and nothing else. Continue to do this for five minutes. If your mind drifts off to any other thought besides the sensation of air passing in and out of your body, then just begin again. Go ahead and try it. Observe what your mind does as you attempt this simple task. I'll be waiting for you in the next paragraph when you finish. Incidentally, it is generally easier if you try it with your eyes closed.

Well, how did you do? Come on, be honest.

Chances are very good that you had trouble keeping your mind on the job (or nose) for more than a second or two. It was probably difficult for some of you to get your mind to stay with your breathing for even a second. Your mind had other ideas. Some of the more common ideas: "This is stupid," "Am I doing it right?" "This is boring," "How do you pay attention to breathing?" and/or "This is easy," followed by "Oops!" Making any comment to yourself while attempting to focus on your breathing means your mind was talking to itself rather than observing itself. Likewise, any other stray thoughts or distractions would result in a break in focus. Resting your mental focus upon just one thing is tough to do.

We have all had the experience of having our attention riveted to a good movie or a suspenseful novel. Under highly stimulating conditions, it is easy to tune everything else out except for the movie or book. But that, of course, is really the point of the experiment. Our mind can only stay focused on very strong, external stimuli that are designed specifically to hold our attention. Otherwise, the drunken monkey trips along distracted by this, that and every other thing.

Meditation is the practice of steadily focusing upon one thing only. The object focused upon can be almost anything. The flow of air through the nasal passage is one method; the rising and falling of the abdomen as one breathes is another. In Transcendental Meditation (TM) a sacred sound or "mantra"—such as "om"—is used. Zen Buddhist tradition makes use of confounding statements like "what is the sound of one hand clapping" as well as the breathing exercise described above. A multitude of other approaches are available, some of which will be described below. All meditation techniques, however, have one thing in common: the training of attention so it stays where we put it. In this way, the drunken monkey gradually sobers up.

Breathing Lessons

A great number of meditation techniques are based upon the observation of one's own breathing. Breathing, after all, is one of our most basic physiological functions. We take about 18 breaths per minute, or about 9½ million breaths a year. Our bodies are totally dependent upon the steady supply of oxygen and release of carbon dioxide. Yet there is a more subtle aspect to breathing. If we look at the origin of the words "respiration" and "expiration" we find the root word "spiritus" which means "to breathe." Perhaps, then, our breath is the vehicle upon which the Spirit rides.

The "in-spiration" meditation technique is based upon an appreciation of the relationship between breathing and spirituality. Quite simply, in this technique you are not just breathing in air or oxygen; you are bathing your body with love, light and spiritual energy. Conversely, each exhalation is releasing any toxicity or negativity from your body that it may have. In with the good vibes, out with the bad. While it is true that normal, nonmeditative breathing has the quality of vitalizing and detoxifying the body (see what happens if you don't breathe—you'll get real toxic in about a minute), if you focus your attention upon the spiritual significance of the "re-spiratory" cycle, additional benefits may follow.

To practice this particular meditation you need to turn your attention to the flow of air in and out of your body. Follow the air as it passes through your nose, into your lungs, then into your bloodstream and finally on to various parts of your body. Because oxygen is whisked throughout your entire body, you might systematically *imagine* the air as it travels within you. Likewise, as you exhale, appreciate the fact that your body is being relieved of all physical and emotional toxicity.

Remember: The key element in all meditation is the focusing of attention. Regardless of the technique used, the mind will have other ideas. It will probably not stay where you put it for very long. It will be easily distracted. That's okay. Just keep dragging it back gently, patiently, lovingly. Try this particular meditation right now for five or ten minutes and then we'll look at some of the problems that may have occurred.

Did you try the meditation for at least five minutes? No? Well I'm not letting you read any further until you do. Now go on, meditate!

Okay. Your mind kept straying off in a thousand and one different directions, you got a slight tension headache, you almost dozed off and then fell asleep. Good morning! Or did you decide to quit before the five minutes were up! Tsk, tsk. That's okay; you're not the only one. Let's examine some of these obstacles to see what might be done about them.

Housebreaking Your Mind

Have you ever paper-trained a puppy? Every time the puppy runs off the newspaper you just patiently bring it back onto the paper. It generally takes quite a while for the puppy to get the idea of what is expected of him, and so it takes considerable patience on the part of the trainer. So it is with your mind. You must be patient. Every time you find that your mind has gone off on some journey without your permission or consent, just be patient and gently return your attention to the object of your meditation. It's as if you say to yourself, "that (the thing that distracted you) is interesting, but that's not what I'm focusing on right now." As a more experienced meditator, you may want to take note of what distracted you, but in the beginning it is probably best to just get back on track.

Get Comfortable

Meditation as it is practiced in the USA was imported from India and Japan. Originally in these countries only the very wealthy had chairs; this is why meditating has come to be known as something that must be done while sitting cross-legged on the floor. Sitting cross-legged while meditating is like eating Chinese food with chopsticks—a nice idea maybe, but it has nothing to do with the taste of the food.

It is best to simply find a comfortable position that allows you to sit for a while without physical distractions or pain. Don't get too comfortable or you might nod off. Catching the Dreamland Express is okay if a beauty rest is your goal, but as a meditation exercise it's a total bust. The best approach may be sitting in a straight-backed chair with your spine relatively straight. For those who are so inclined, however, meditative practices can be joined with different postural alignments through the study of yoga. "Yoga" means "yoking" of mind and body.

Easy Does It

Many people stop meditating because they experience discomfort. One reason is trying too hard. Ideally, a state of *relaxed attentiveness* should be cultivated while meditating. Getting enlightened in just a few days is simply out of the question, so ease off. Indeed, it is precisely this "fast food" mentality that will stand in the way of making the kind of progress you want. Greed for fruit misses the flower. A pity. Being there is all the fun. Patiently tune in on the object of your attention. Don't force it.

Don't Fizzle Out

Millions of Americans have purchased memberships at health spas with the sincere intention of working out on a regular basis. Health spas, however, count on only a small fraction of the members actually showing up more than a dozen times or so. There simply wouldn't be enough space if everyone were conscientious about working out. This same tendency to fizzle out after a few sessions also occurs among would-be meditators. The fact that this occurs is especially interesting in that none of the reasons (i.e., excuses) used by spa dropouts applies to meditation. After all, you don't have to go anywhere to practice meditation; your head is always conveniently located on a neck near you! You can't adopt a bad attitude toward the instructor if you don't have one. And you don't even need to feel embarassed about how well or poorly you're doing in your "workouts."

People tend to drop out of meditative practice for one of three reasons: lack of schedule, mental fatigue and failure to pay attention.

Lack Of Schedule

Unless meditation is made part of a regular routine, there will be a powerful tendency to miss a session here and there and after a while, a month or more may go by before you realize that you haven't meditated. For this reason, it's best to set aside a specific period every day to practice. You may only do ten minutes at first. This is plenty for most people.

Eventually you may want to meditate for up to an hour. Some people also recommend meditating several times a day. But consistency is a key to progress in meditative practice.

Mental Fatigue

Just as a physical workout can be exhausting, meditation can be tiring, particularly at first. It may seem as if your mind is out of control; you just want to tell it to "get lost" (actually it already is). Don't give up; there is hope.

Remember when you did push-ups? Or any other form of exercise? The first few repetitions were easy to do, but after a while your muscles began to ache, then burn, then ache some more. It was only the last few that built new muscle. Similarly, in meditation there is great value in practicing for the full ten minutes even if your mind begins to fight you. Feel the burn, baby.

Failure To Pay Attention

While it might not be meditation in its purest form, simply paying attention while you are in an otherwise boring class or meeting, or in any situation where your mind might otherwise wander, is a superb way of tuning your mental focus. Once you begin, you'll be amazed how often you catch your mind floating off into the stratosphere. As you practice, your mental muscle will toughen up and become stronger and more responsive to your direction.

The breathing exercises described above are very basic meditation practices that could keep you busy for several years or more. But breathing isn't for everybody! The following meditation techniques are only a sampling. Many other techniques are described in the books listed in the References section at the back of this book.

The Four Senses Sanctification

This one should be practiced in an environment that is free from people talking or other man-made (or woman-made) sounds, if at all possible. Natural settings such as the woods, the mountains or beside a stream are just perfect.

To practice this meditation, close your eyes and systematically relax various muscle groups, working from head to toes (or vice versa). Just "let go" of any tension and allow yourself to sink down, down, down into a peaceful state of relaxation.

Once you are *loose, limp, lazy* and *relaxed*, tune in to the world of sounds and just listen. Without straining, effortlessly listen. Digest the universe of chirpings, gurglings and other sounds with your ears. Let the sounds fill your consciousness. Imagine that you're trying to get the clearest possible signal on a radio. Let go and keep tuning in on the sound. And then thank your Higher Power for the world of sound and your ability to experience it.

After you've done this for a while, do the same thing with smell (actually, this is your chance to practice the breathing meditation described a few paragraphs back). Continue with the breathing exercise until you've had enough, but be sure to thank God for the breath of life.

Next, let your awareness settle on your hands, feet, face, hair, kidney, heart and wherever else you choose. You can bop around or be systematic about it. But be sure to love your body and thank God for it. Take your time. Get into your kidneys, your spleen and, of course, your beautiful brain. Get microscopic. Get small. Become an atom casually floating through your body. Feel the ground holding you, supporting you. Notice the breeze as it lovingly caresses you.

Finally, open your eyes and enjoy the visual feast. Again, thank God for your eyes and the world of colors.

This meditation can have the effect of "cleansing" four of the primary sensory channels through which you experience the world. As your sensory channels get more finely tuned, your experience of the world may begin to change for you in some very satisfying ways.

Meditating On Food

Take an orange and get the feel of it in your hands; notice its texture, weight and firmness. Take time to experience this fruit in a new way. Slow down. Examine minutely its skin and color. As you peel it, notice the smell and the sounds, one sensory channel at a time. Smell it. Rub it against your face, your lips, your tongue.

Now, take a single wedge and eat it s-l-o-w-l-y. Notice the tiny cells of juice that make up each wedge. Take the smallest piece of this wedge and taste it. Close your eyes and make love to it with your taste buds. And thank God for this fruit as you eat it.

Similarly, take the time to eat a meal with this same level of sensitivity and awareness. If you do this periodically, you are likely to experience at least three benefits as indirect by-products. First, you will end up eating more slowly and become satisfied on significantly less food. Second, your selection of foods may become healthier. Finally, food may become simply food again rather than the symbol of love it currently may be.

Om, Om On The Range . . .

The repetition of a phrase or "sacred sound" (such as the mantra "om") is perhaps the most ancient form of meditation. But it is not necessary to use weird baby-talk phrases from foreign lands. You can use your own weird baby-talk phrases if you want. The sounds you choose can be real words or nonsense syllables, such as boogie woogie wa wa doo.

On the other hand, you might prefer to use meaningful phrases such as "one day at a time," "love," "peace," "God," "God is Love," or maybe just "one," as in oneness with God and humankind. You get the idea; you can make up your own. In using a meaningful phrase, allow your mind to dwell upon the essence of the word or phrase for a period of time as you repeat it. As your mind drifts off onto some related or unrelated matter, just bring your attention back to the phrase. This is more properly referred to as "contemplation."

Along a slightly different line, repeating "I love you (your own name)" a hundred times or so is a very powerful mantra with great healing qualities. Try this one for a week or so. It's difficult to do without feeling good. As one of God's creations, you are certainly worthy of your love. So tell yourself so: "I love you. I love you. Yes. I love you."

In The Hands Of God

A meditation to practice while lying in bed at night is imagining that you're lying in the hand of God. That you're resting, completely supported in this large, soft, all-powerful hand. And that this hand supports you, comforts you and cradles you like a loving father or mother. Hold that image in your mind as you fall asleep at night.

Prayer As A Spiritual Practice

Remembering what we said a little earlier about the fallacy of seeing God as a cosmic bellhop. I'd like to borrow a suggestion from the 12-Step fellowships. Specifically, the 11th Step recommends praying only for knowledge of God's will and the power to carry it out.

When we ask God to do something or tell God what needs doing (such as helping our team win, since God loves our team better than theirs!), we are putting ourselves in God's place. If we were that smart, of course, we wouldn't have to turn to God in the first place. Imagining that we can put the word out into the universe and have the world respond to our whims is very superstitious and what psychologists call magical thinking. If taken to the extreme—believing that our thinking of something makes it so—we have the stuff of which psychosis is made.

There is an order to the universe as revealed by the laws of physics, chemistry, biology and other known natural laws (and some yet unknown). By praying for knowledge of God's will for us, we may be able to get a hint of our place in that order and a sense of what we can do to solve our dilemmas.

A prayer technique worth trying is to imagine that your heart is a sensory organ, that it can actually hear. Imagine that there's actually a hinge and a door on your heart, and that you're opening that door when you pray: "God, what do you want me to do?" Your mind can become still enough to hear that quiet inner voice—the deeper wisdom that is available to us.

To make sure you're not just listening to your own selfish wishes, it's always wise to talk to other people whose opinions you respect, who are objective and who have your own well-being at heart. Seek out their opinions, because it's clear that God does talk through other people.

Once you've obtained a sense of what God's will is, you could try asking God to help you carry it out. "If this is your will for me, help me to do it." A compulsive overeater might thus become aware that it is God's will for her to abstain from refined sugar and white flour, and then ask daily (or hourly) for help in remaining abstinent.

In this way, prayer is not to fulfill some egocentric quest, but rather to bring oneself into harmony with this larger reality.

Repetition is very useful in prayer. While practice may not make you perfect, it may improve your praying. If you practice meditation only once a month and shoot up a prayer only in case of emergency, you're not as likely to get that cozy comfortable feeling of conscious contact with God experienced by those who have integrated prayer and mediation into their daily life.

Prayer several times a day—even if it's just a few minutes in the morning, afternoon and evening—will help you develop a spiritual consciousness. Be gentle in this quest. The person who wants to be at one with God and demands it *now* is likely to have a life that's more self-centered than God-centered. The attitude that seems to work best is easy does it, but do it.

Affirmations

An affirmation is, in a sense, a reaching toward God. An affirmation is the statement of a desired condition as if that condition had already been achieved. For example, one affirmation might be: "I am a perfect child of God" or "I am a child of God and the universe supports me and heals my body and makes it function perfectly." The idea is that if we put our desired state into our consciousness, it will eventually manifest itself. There is some evidence that this positive attitude has a beneficial effect on our immune systems and the healthy functioning of our bodies.

We human beings are constantly talking to ourselves: it is part of our basic nature. Unfortunately, lovesick individuals don't talk very positively. For a variety of reasons, we have developed a habit of being self-critical. When something goes wrong we may call ourselves "stupid," and when something goes right we say we were "just lucky."

Our words are like magic wands. What we say to ourselves directly affects the results we get in life. The purpose of using affirmations is to correct our tendency to be negative and self-abusive.

Here are some affirmations you might try or adapt to suit your particular situation. Say or write each affirmation slowly six to ten times in a row, several times a day. Some of the best times to repeat your affirmations are in the morning and at bedtime. Another good time is when you are stuck in traffic! At first your old, negative self may resist these affirmations: your negative self prefers nah-firmations! With practice, however, this resistance will disappear.

- I am confident. My conscience is clear and my life is secure.
- I deserve love and I have love to share with others.
- I am a perfect child of God with a special purpose.
- I am comfortable with other people and am open to trying new ways of being.
- I am an honest, lovable person.
- I now forgive and release the past. I am open to miracles in my life today.
- I have special gifts from God.

Several books are identified in the Resource section of this book for those interested in utilizing affirmations as part of their prayer life.

Other Spiritual Practices

Daily Devotions

Other things that can help spiritual growth are reading literature of a spiritual nature. Most bookstores carry numerous books of daily meditations and daily prayers. There are some books that address spirituality from the Judeo-Christian tradition, some that are associated with the

New Thought movement, some that are integrated with 12-Step philosophies and are directed to individuals with special needs, such as those recovering from alcoholism, compulsive overeating, co-dependency and so on. Other books of affirmations draw from various traditions that are thousands of years old, yet have messages as modern as today. Reading such spiritual literature may help you develop your own spiritual philosophy.

Spiritual Retreats

Another option is going on spiritual retreats. For many people, particularly those stuck in a rut or those just beginning to develop their beliefs, retreats are helpful in making spiritual progress. These retreats are often sponsored by mainstream religions or spiritual organizations. They may last a single day or more than a week.

Stick with retreats offered by well-established organizations that charge a fair rate and do not promise instant enlightenment. Retreats are a wonderful time to get away from the telephone, the newspaper and the TV and from the other stresses and strains of daily life. They're an excellent way of jump-starting your spiritual growth and improving your conscious contact with God. There are some manipulative groups, however, who use retreats to gain control over you and your cash. So choose wisely.

Spiritual Consciousness

To be fully effective, spiritual practices can't be saved for private moments; they must be incorporated into daily life. For example, consider the concept of "turning it over." Frequently we find ourselves facing a situation which we really and truly *can do nothing* about, which we can only turn over to God. A few years ago, I was facing a severe downturn in my professional life. The treatment centers I had started were on the verge of bankruptcy. We had lost half a million dollars in a day as a result of some poor business decisions. We were faced with the possibility of having to lay off some staff or folding our tents and going off into the sunset. This was particularly painful for me because I had deep affection for the people I was working with, let alone the clients who were enrolled in our program. It was then that I remembered the concept of *turning it over.*

It happened to me while sitting in a dentist's chair, waiting for the novocaine to numb my jaw. I was ruminating about what to do, what to do, what to do. I wanted to escape. I wanted to hide. I wanted to go to the Cayman Islands and sell ice cream on the beach. And then it hit me. I had done everything I could to straighten things out. There was absolutely nothing else I could do—except turn it over to God. For me this meant saying: "God, I've done all I can. If you want these treatment centers to continue, and if you want me to continue to do this work, fine. If you don't, fine. I'm just gonna keep on doing what I can till I get some news or signs from you about what my next steps should be." I hadn't had a whiff of laughing gas, yet I started to laugh. I knew it was no longer just in my hands. And I knew, really and truly knew, regardless of how things actually went, that all would be fine. And it was.

From that moment on, my mind was not preoccupied with the dread of it all. Rather, I had an inner sense that things were going to work out. I should add that there was no objective evidence whatsoever that this was true. As it turned out, in short order things did turn out well. In fact, they were better than ever. However, at that moment in the dentist's chair, I was comfortable with the idea that even if my treatment centers had to close, it would be okay not just for me but for my clients and the people who were working with me.

I had to do the footwork, but once that was done all I could do was turn the rest over to God. I'm responsible for the effort but I have no control over the results. For many of us, our natural tendency is to expect the worst in any difficult situation. When you're in a hole, all you can think is that you'll never get out. That's because we have a limited view, and we don't have access to the big picture. For this reason, there's an enormous psychological benefit to turning things over to a higher power—or Higher Power. Having made the effort, I then say, "It's in your hands. I've done all I can. It's yours now."

Another spiritual concept is to "fake it 'til you make it." The idea is to act as if there is a God regardless of whether you think there is or isn't. You're not going to be able to prove the existence of God, so fake it! Pray and live life as if there is a divine being who has a concern for our well being and see how it works out. Famed psychologist Alfred Adler called that fictional finalism: if we live our lives *as if* a certain condition exits, a self-fulfilling prophecy gets activated and we may actually receive the benefits that come with having those thoughts.

Bad Things Happen

Finally, I'd like to talk about one of the other major obstacles that many people have with the concept of God or a Higher Power—the undeniable fact that bad things happen to good people. The death of a child, rape or murder of a loved one, illness that takes a mother or father from his or her children, wars, famine, pestilence, poverty—how does one reconcile all these things with the concept of a God that loves us unconditionally?

We've already said that the expectation of using prayer to achieve miraculous cures and divine intervention is not a viable one. I should add that there are those who disagree, but I can't say that I've witnessed any divine interventions. Spirituality does, however, give a different perspective to how one experiences life.

Take illness, for example. For the person who is facing a terminal illness or a physically limiting one, the first question is how could God do this? How could there be a God that would allow me to become a father only to leave my children in financial hardship?

Theologians have a couple of answers. One is the old story of Job, whose loyalty and steadfastness were tested by God, who inflicted on him a series of personal disasters. The punch line in the story of Job is that we humans can't possibly understand the ways of God; there is a purpose to everything that happens but we're not quite up to hearing the whole story. In other words, bad stuff happens. Our own earthly interpretation of misfortune is that it is terribly unfair. Perhaps after we die we will have a better understanding of the larger picture, the big design.

Another answer, sometimes too glibly offered, is that good can come from suffering. Members of A.A., for example, sometimes say they are grateful for being an alcoholic because now they have become part of a loving fellowship which they would never have found otherwise. That's nice to say, but wait a minute. Why didn't God just drop your butt down in a loving community from the very beginning and skip all the dry heaves, DTs and broken marriages?

The best explanation of evil that I've ever heard came from Nobel prize-winning author Elie Wiesel. He tells a story that takes place in a concentration camp in Nazi Germany. Within this concentration camp an atheist and a man who's very religious have an ongoing argument about whether God exists. One day, a young boy is caught by the Nazis stealing a loaf of bread, and the Nazis decide to teach the prisoners in the camp a lesson by having a public hanging of that boy. So all the prisoners are brought out into the yard where the hanging is to take place. The young boy is dragged up onto the scaffold and the noose is placed over his head. The executioner tightens the noose around the boy's neck and then pulls the trap door. The boy falls through the door and all the camp prisoners are forced to watch as the boy kicks and swings by his neck.

But the boy doesn't die. Because his body is so light, the knot on the noose fails to snap his neck. The executioner hauls the boy back up, pulling him up by the rope around his neck. Once again, with the knot tighter now, the trap door is sprung and the boy falls, yet the boy's neck still fails to snap. He swings and chokes, but does not die. They pull him back up a second time and tie weights to his legs, thus ensuring that this time his neck will snap and he will die. For a third time the trap door is opened, and this time the boy falls through and his neck snaps. Finally, he dies.

Throughout this horrible proceeding, the atheist is standing beside the religious man. In disgust, he turns to the religious man and asks, "So tell me, where is your God now?" And the religious man says: "Where is he? It's quite obvious, isn't it? He's up there hanging by his neck."

God may be the life force but God needs our help to help make things right. God suffers right along with us. There are all sorts of horrible things on this planet. There is unnecessary pain and suffering. But because we are a piece of God that is conscious of itself, we not only have the capacity to see how imperfect life is, we have the capacity to work toward eliminating these imperfections. We have cured illness. We can end famine and reduce man's inhumanity to man. If this were an ideal world committed to doing God's will, we would devote the resources that are now used to build bombs and accumulateg wealth to doing all those things that need to be done. It is possible that we are God's feet and hands and brain. To the degree that we don't work to eliminate suffering, God suffers. And we suffer.

If we can step back far enough, we can see that in fact progress has been made. It is, after all, an evolutionary process, and it takes time. The average life expectancy used to be 30 years, now it's 70. Inherent in evolution is a greater awareness of injustice and inequities. There was polio, and we've pretty much stamped that out. For eons there were various forms of slavery, but today it is almost gone.

The human species is maybe a million years old, but this thing called civilization began only 5,000 to 7,000 years ago. It's only during those last few thousand years that we've been engaged in a dialogue about what's right and wrong.

We're that part of God that's able to ask those kinds of questions. We are the latest version of God's image. And the more we love and cultivate a loving image of God, the more love there will be.

CHAPTER 6

TALKING TO OURSELVES

While God, as we understand Him, is the primary source of unconditional love, we ourselves run a close second. Before we can rely on ourselves as a dependable source of support, we have to change, which is not easy. That's why we're devoting two chapters to it, this one and the next.

Someone has said we are "languaging animals." We communicate with each other more than any other animals. But it isn't enough that we talk to each other; we also talk to ourselves.

We are constantly making comments to ourselves about the events in our life. And contrary to what we may have been told when we were younger, it is perfectly normal to talk to ourselves. Everyone does it. Mostly we do it subvocally. That is, we talk to ourselves in the form of thoughts.

As you drive along in your car, on your way to work, a conversation is going on in your mind. Perhaps you are preparing a "things to do" list. Maybe you are rehashing an argument you had with a co-worker the day before. Regardless of the content or circumstances, your mind is constantly processing the raw data of life by translating every event into an internal, private narration.

Of all the things that we talk with ourselves about, one of the most popular topics is our *selves.*

Most of the time we are consciously unaware of the things we say to ourselves. Unless you intentionally try to listen in to your "self-talk," you won't even know what you've been saying about yourself. It's as if you were talking behind your back. The nerve of you!

For most people, but especially individuals addicted to lovesickness, this subconcious chatter tends to be negative. We say things like: "Geez, Bob, you really blew it this time." "Bob, you know that was really a stupid thing to do." This probably has a lot to do with the notion that if we are critical of ourselves, we'll behave better. We believe that these harangues are needed to help us do better next time. It's as if a football coach dashes into the locker room at half time and delivers a dressing-down to us in order to turn around a losing game.

Individuals who are trapped in addiction habitually engage in these endless bursts of self-criticism. The morning-after acts of contrition never stop: "You idiot! Never, never again. I would rather kill myself. That's it, you jerk. Oh, brother, What a loser I am," and so on. Anyone who has engaged in such verbal tirades knows that they simply have no lasting effect on us at all.

Kicking Ourselves

Short-term assaults on ourselves work. I may want so badly to change my behavior that I will buck up and work harder, at least for a little while. But because these criticisms are attacks on our self, ultimately they leave us feeling just a little worse. We undermine ourselves and then we become dependent upon further self-criticism to get ourselves motivated once again. We think we need to give ourselves a kick in the rear to get going, but we don't stay on the straight and narrow for very long. On an unconscious level, our minds follow a logical sequence that runs something like this:

1. "I'm a rotten, lazy, stupid slug for doing ______________ ______________." (Fill in the blank with some destructive

behavior which you are trying to eliminate with critical self-attacks).

2. "Because I'm a rotten, lazy, stupid slug, I may as well do what rotten, lazy, stupid slugs do."

3. "What do rotten, lazy, stupid slugs do? They ___________ _______________." (Fill in the blank with the same destructive behavior which we're trying to eliminate in the first place with these critical self-attacks.)

Oh brother, how exhausting. And how disrespectful of ourselves, and damaging, too. It's one thing to acknowledge a lapse or mistake; it's another to keep on punishing yourself day in and day out on the grounds that those lapses and mistakes make you a bad person. You try to correct mistakes, but you also have to realize that you can't totally eliminate them. Human beings are fallible; there's nothing we can do about that. What we can do is stop punishing ourselves for being human. Just because you have violated some sacred rule doesn't mean you have to suffer. You made a mistake, *but you yourself aren't a mistake.*

There's an entire branch of psychology and psychotherapy devoted to helping people see the relationship between their self-criticism and feelings. Quite simply, it is that your feelings about yourself are determined by what you say to yourself. If you feel lousy, it is because you've been terrorizing yourself with harassing comments.

One thing you might ask yourself is this: "If being self-critical was so successful, why am I not perfect by now?" Chances are you've been criticizing yourself since you were two years old. You've probably been critical of every possible behavior. How many of those behaviors have disappeared? Has self-criticism helped you find what you were looking for or has it only dug you a deeper hole?

Possibly there are some short-term gains, but more than likely it has become clear that, lo and behold, the same basic character problems are still there.

It's worth noting that most self-destructive behaviors were developed for a reason. They served a function at sometime in our lives. We were doing the best we could at the time. Rather than berate ourselves, instead we should acknowledge that the current behaviors simply no longer work for us. They seemed like a good idea at one time, but no longer do the trick.

We'll Fix Joe

To demonstrate why we should knock off the negative self-talk, let's take Joe Happiness, the guy who won the Mental Health Olympics. Pretend we take this serene and peaceful guy and surgically implant tiny loudspeakers into his ears. Then we stereophonically play a tape that repeats things like: "You're a loser. You're a failure. You've screwed up. If people really knew the truth about you they wouldn't like you," and on and on, hour after hour, day after day. If we keep this steady barrage of negativity going for even a few days, this healthiest of all healthy human beings will soon become depressed and pessimistic. He may begin drinking heavily and engage in other escape behaviors. It won't be long before he wants to do himself in.When people use a gun to commit suicide, most of them shoot themselves in the head, perhaps to finally turn off all that negative chatter.

You can't learn to love yourself by spouting hate to yourself. Hating yourself won't make you more lovable!

Addictions and self-destructive tendencies grow in an atmosphere of self-hate. Negativity is the essential nutrient that these behavior patterns thrive upon.

Well-meaning people taught some of us that it was unhealthy to be proud of ourselves. ("Remember, dear, pride goeth before a fall!") They said pride would produce arrogance and self-centeredness. They said be modest, be humble and never take credit. That's all well and good for the person who *has a healthy sense of self.*

Don't get me wrong. Modesty and humility grease the wheels of interpersonal relationships with family, friends, and colleagues. It's important to be a team member, at home and at work.

However, there is a distinction between interpersonal relationships (your relationships with others) and intrapersonal relationships (your relationship with yourself). In the relationship with yourself, you need to give yourself credit—absolute unconditional self-love.

If You Can't Say Something Nice . . .

The first step in learning to talk lovingly to yourself involves stopping self-criticism. Although it may take a little while to make progress in reducing your self-critical nature, and although you may never do it perfectly, you should be able to make progress if you practice the following suggestions:

1. ***Listen To Yourself.*** Begin noticing what you are saying to yourself. Examine your thoughts while in bed late at night or first thing in the morning. Pay attention and you'll see what you really think of yourself.

2. ***Be Gentle With Yourself.*** As you are likely to discover, you can be extremely harsh with yourself. Even if you think you deserve every nasty thing you say to yourself, make a commitment to take it easy on yourself. Be gentle. Imagine that inside you there is a vulnerable child who is scared and looking for protection. Quit frightening your inner child.

3. ***Don't Criticize Your Critical Self.*** You don't deserve condemnation just because you have a self-critical nature. Don't criticize yourself for being critical of yourself. Just take it easy. Notice the fact that you've been critical of yourself, then knock it off. It's okay to criticize your behavior. If you're habitually late for appointments, for instance, you can take note of that and do something to remind yourself to start earlier. But quit criticizing yourself.

4. ***Distract Yourself.*** Sometimes you may fall into a negative rut, particularly after you have screwed up a project or caused pain to someone. As a sensitive person, you may feel these things more deeply than others. Instead of berating yourself endlessly, an effective strategy is to seek relief through a number of distractions.

   I'm often the oldest kid in the video arcade. These games thoroughly grab my attention and completely derail any train of thought I may be stuck with. I go to arcades to get out of my rut. My other distractions are going to the movies, reading a good book, playing my saxophone, working out and listening to my favorite music on my headphones.

   You need to find your own distractions. They ought to be activities that don't involve speaking. The trick is to get out of the language mode—to lose your mind. Most destructive behavior patterns do this by either seducing or sedating our brains. The challenge is to find a half-dozen or so healthy ways to achieve the same effect.

5. ***Be Patient.*** Your lousy self-image wasn't built overnight and it won't be remodeled that quickly, either. You're in this process for the long haul; don't be disappointed if the results come more slowly than you'd hoped. That's just more of your overly-demanding, perfectionist, self-criticism! So lighten up. Easy does it.

Whisper Sweet Somethings In Your Ear

I've been working on it for over ten years and I don't mind admitting that my brain still trashes itself from time to time. This is an ancient behavior pattern that's rooted deeply in our earliest experiences. It may even have biological roots. I wouldn't be surprised if I never shake it altogether. In the meantime, however, I've been successful at reducing the time my brain festers on my imperfections.

Simultaneous with the reduction of self-assaults should be the introduction of *sweet somethings*. Begin to speak to yourself as if you were someone you loved.

What do you say to those you love? You tell them how wonderful they are, how much you enjoy their company and, of course, you say, "I love you."

Given the fact that we are always talking to ourselves, why not speak to ourselves in the nicest possible way? For most people, this means saying: "I love you."

Say to yourself, "I love you, ____________________ (your own name), I love you, ____________________, I love you, ____________________," until your jaw gets tired. I recommend giving yourself at least one hundred "I love you's" a day. You can say them while you're brushing your teeth in the morning, while you're in the shower, while you're driving to work or whenever you have a spare minute. Shower your mind in "I love you's." Smooch, smooch!

Don't get hung up on the idea of doing exactly a hundred of them. Concentrate instead on the idea of making this self-love a new rhythm in your mind.

Right now hundreds of thousands, perhaps millions of

people, are walking around listening to a repetitious pattern of thought that goes something like this: "I'm a loser. I'm a failure. I'm a phony. I'm a fake. Life sucks and it's never going to get any better."

This tune is playing over and over in their minds, but it can be replaced with a new one: "I love you, Horace," "I love you, Jonathan," "I love you, Samantha," or whatever your name is.

It has been suggested that the mind is like a computer that is programmed to function according to certain prescribed rules. Most of us are programmed with far too much self-criticism. We need to reprogram ourselves with gentle, loving logic. The key to overcoming our old programming is repetition. In with the good messages, out with the bad—repeatedly.

This simple trick—saying "I love you, Bob"—has been incredibly effective in relieving the insecurity which so many of us feel. You can give yourself "I love you's" with passionate intensity or with absolutely no emotion whatsoever. Say them mechanically and they will have the same impact because you're putting the thoughts through your nervous system, into your consciousness.

Write Yourself A Love Letter

Another way to give yourself loving approval is to write love letters. Set some time aside to write your self a love letter or, better yet, a poem. Be lavish and exaggerate your love. An example of such a letter might be:

> To my most beloved:
>
> I am taking a few moments to let you know how very important you are to me. More than anything or anyone else in the world, I love you. I cherish you. I know that I can't possibly live without you. You are a perfect expression of everything I could ever hope for. The ideal human being. I love you, and I always will.

If there is someone whose love you have particularly hoped for, imagine that they wrote the letter. It's okay. The important thing is to put the loving language through your nervous system repeatedly. Writing and reading such loving stuff involves you more thoroughly than simply saying "I love you," so why not add love notes to your new romance?

Through The Looking Glass Lovingly

My next suggestion is that you get married.

Get married to yourself. One of the most powerful techniques I know is to marry the mirror. Write a marriage vow to yourself as if you actually, really and truly were going to marry you.

Here's an example of a simple marriage vow (though you should have fun making up your own):

> I love you __________(your own name) and I will do everything I can to take care of you forever. No matter what happens, in good times as well as bad, in sickness and in health, I will always be there for you. I love you and nothing will ever change my mind. You are the most important person in my life. Without you, I am nobody. I love you. And I always will love you.

Having written our marriage vows, it's now time to go ahead and get married! Now I've never liked large weddings. My suggestion is that you elope with yourself in the privacy of your own home. It would be interesting to say your vows before a crowd of relatives and friends, but that's likely to get you a one-way ticket to a mental institution, too. (Then again, if they knew what you were up to, it might be beneficial. Hmmm?)

So, assuming you're going solo with this self-marriage, stand in front of a mirror with your vows memorized. Look at yourself as if you were looking at another human being. Most of the time when we look in the mirror, we are merely inspecting our hair, makeup, ear hairs or whatever. This time, be fully aware of yourself standing face-to-face with you. All of you. Your best and your worst qualities. Your future and your past. Your fantasies and your fears. Perhaps you could do it naked if you've got a problem with your body image.

Standing or sitting before the mirror, take a minute or two to contemplate what you are about to do. You are about to make a lifelong commitment that might very well change your life. Invite God to stand in as your witness.

Once you have overcome the thoughts about how weird, silly and awkward the whole scene is, proceed with reciting or reading your vows to your *self.* Go slowly. Say each word in such a way that your mind can fully wrap around the meaning of what you are saying.

Once you are done, you are likely to feel a range of emotions: embarrassment, love, nausea, silliness. Regardless of what you feel, don't worry about it. It's too late now, you're married!

When I face particularly difficult challenges in my professional or personal life or when I'm going into a stressful meeting where my feelings of insecurity are likely to surface, I'll stop in the men's room beforehand and look in the mirror. If I'm alone, I might even speak out loud; if people are around, I'll just take some time, wash my face, look in the mirror and pretend that I'm combing my hair. I'm really renewing my vows. I'm telling me that I love me, giving myself love, attention, acceptance, affection, and committing myself to me.

Music To Your Ears

Another option is to make a tape recording of "I love you, ____________." Play it in your car on the way to work. I have this fantasy about filling an auditorium with people and having them shout out repeatedly: "We love you, Bob, we love you, Bob!" Over and over, the crowd would wildly roar in exaltation their undying love for me. How nice.

They're Singing Your Song

If there's a love song that's got your name in it, get a copy and play it frequently. Create a tape that plays the song over and over again so that you can just pop it in and sing along with it whenever you need a dose of love.

Affirmations

Make sure some of the affirmations talked about in Chapter 5 are aimed at loving you. Check the Resources section at the back of this book for ideas.

Little White Lies

In my work as a therapist with addicted individuals, I frequently encounter folks who protest: "I can't say that I love myself because I don't. It would be a lie." Suddenly hardcore dope-fiends suffer an attack of integrity! The truth is that many people deeply stuck in a mode of self-hate find it very difficult to talk nicely to themselves.

If that's true of you, try using another voice. In my own experience, there was a young woman who had dumped me and whose love I still badly wanted. She used to say she loved me. When I couldn't manage to feel any love for myself, I'd invoke memories of her voice and play her "I love you, Bob" over and over in my mind. I didn't think for one moment that she'd come back or that she actually loved me. But the memory of her saying so was just what I needed to get my mental tape playing, to get the message running in my head.

One client lost his mother at an early age and he didn't have any memory of her saying, "I love you," to him, In his mind he imagined her voice and invoked images of her saying this to him.

Another option is to imagine the "I love you" coming directly from God. This is an affirmative meditation, one that can quickly become comforting—the love of God.

The Truth Feels Good

In the larger scheme of things, it's a lie to say that you're a loser and that you are unlovable. The truth is that you are a unique human being, the only one of your kind, an incredible creation of the universe, made in the image of God. A negative self-evaluation is generally based on some very small, superficial things that pale in comparison to your potential and your essential goodness. And that's the truth!

By the way, people who are *really* rotten never think they are. The fact you've been so critical of yourself shows you do care and essentially are a good person. Your problem is that in trying to be better you're too hard on yourself. Regardless of what your mind says about you, act as if you deserve your love because you do.

A Harmless Experiment

If you're telling yourself that all this hocus pocus about marrying a mirror and pretending to fall in love with yourself won't work for you, don't worry. You're normal. We all think we're too smart for con jobs, particularly those that we pull on ourselves. But one thing you can do is think of this as an experiment. Do the "I love you" exercise for a week or so and see if it doesn't begin to change the quality of how you feel on a day-to-day basis. Don't expect it to work. That's okay. Just follow the instructions and see what happens. It's a harmless experiment, that's all.

But don't be surprised if something does happen. A lot of people experience improvement in their mood and in their feelings about themselves after a one-week exercise in saying "I love you" one hundred times a day.

Making Deposits In Your Love Account

If you suffer from lovesickness and have a damaged self-image, in the beginning each "I love you" that you give yourself will be worth almost nothing. If we don't think much of ourselves, we don't place much value on our own love.

Think of your "I love yous" as deposits in a love account—kind of like a bank account of your soul. In the beginning, each "I love you" has the equivalent value of about half a cent. Not much, really.

However, if you make a hundred deposits a day, every day, eventually the balance in your "love account" will astound you. As your love account begins to accumulate a surplus of love (and it will), each "I love you" now has greater value because you've got love in the bank and therefore plenty to give. You value yourself more with every investment you make.

Writing Bad Checks

Many lovesick people offer love to others in the hope that they will get love back in return. It's like writing a check on a love account without sufficient funds to cover it. You can't give away what you don't have. If you don't have love for yourself, you can't give it away. You can give sex. You can give money. You can give your neediness. But you can't give love.

It often happens that after trying to give love through some selfless sacrifice, we end up disappointed because the object of our affections didn't return the favor or didn't properly appreciate what we had done. When this happens, the usual reaction is to pout and throw a temper tantrum. If our partner is healthy enough, eventually he or she will walk away.

Far better to invest in ourselves, say "I love you" to ourselves and forget about trying to manipulate somebody else.

Emotional bankruptcy

As an addictions therapist, I've spoken with approximately a thousand people who've relapsed. Interestingly, with very rare exceptions, I have found that almost every addict who relapsed said the same thing beforehand. Whether they were heroin addicts or food addicts, they all said: "To hell with it," or, "f___ it," or the equivalent just prior to the relapse.

When that happens, it's apparent that these people have run out of self-love and no longer care for themselves. They see themselves as having given and given and given of themselves and have nothing left to give. They've exhausted what little self-love was stored away and, now that it's spent, they are emotionally bankrupt. They no longer have the will or strength to invest further in their recovery. "It's just not *worth* it," they say to themselves.

The "I love you's" are investments in one's self. With sufficient "deposits" the lovesick addict develops enough self-worth to continue caring for himself.

Gotta Have Somebody

Many folks may mentally agree with what I'm saying, but deep down inside they still want someone else to love them. They still want that romantic bliss and union with another person.

If you don't love yourself, whoever you do attract is eventually going to catch on to that fact. You can't expect anyone to love you more than you do. You may swap neediness (as so many do), but it ain't love and it won't produce much satisfaction. If you can't love yourself, why should they?

Love yourself and others will join you.

Coasting

Most people do not keep up with their deposits of "I love you's." People will keep it up for a short while but sooner or later they slack off because either a) they don't feel the earth open up and lift them off into a state of saintly self-actualization and so they give up or b) they do feel the earth open up and lift them off into a state of saintly self-actualization, so they think they don't need to practice the self-love any longer. They begin to coast.

As the saying goes, you can only coast if you're going downhill. Practicing self-love has been tested on hundreds of individuals and is based upon a broad spectrum of psychological theory. But it only works if you work it.

Love Yourself Even Though . . .

Most of the people I've worked with have been willing to love themselves *after* they got a promotion, *after* they won the prize, or *after* they have love from somebody else. The problem with doing this is that it is just more *conditional* self-love. Any time you love yourself *because* of something means that you're loving yourself conditionally. What happens to your self-esteem and lovesickness when you don't win the next prize, when you fail? It's okay to love yourself after you've done well; that's fine, but don't bank on it. Don't let that be the basis for loving yourself. The idea is to love yourself unconditionally.

The time that you need your own love the most is when you have screwed up, when you have failed and when you would normally be critical.

For example, suppose you have decided that you wanted to stop eating cookies and cakes, and other fattening foods and Day 1 into your new commitment, you're walking through the mall and the House of Cookies deviously has fans set up next to the ovens so that the smell of freshly baked chocolate chip macademia nut cookies surprisingly wafts toward your nostrils.

Your lovesick, addictive brain says to you: "I'm not going to eat any of these cookies myself, but just because I'm not going to eat them doesn't mean that the kids at home shouldn't be able to have a few." So you buy a small three-pound bag.

The next thing your mind says—and it's probably no surprise to anyone—is this: "Well, eating just one cookie would be okay; just as long as I limit it to one. Or maybe two. Certainly no more than three. Yes, three is the limit. Besides, that book I'm reading has been telling me to love myself anyway, so maybe having that cookie will be an act of self-love." You eat the cookie and immediately shame, guilt and self-criticism begin stomping on your poor fragile ego, and that little voice inside starts saying things like, "You weak-willed worm, you blew it, you suckered yourself again."

What typically happens to most people after violating some rule they've set up for themselves is that the guilt and shame become so great that they dig even deeper into their addictive pattern. To handle the feelings of shame they eat more, and one cookie turns into five or ten. And then they get depressed.

Having violated their "diet," they decide they may as well really overdo it. They eat so much that they get sick—a suitable punishment—and so it goes.

The alternative is to love yourself *anyway*. What is eating all those cookies about in the first place? Certainly it's not to feed a physical hunger. It's feeding an emotional hunger. If we had banked enough "I love you's," the need to eat that first cookie wouldn't have been so strong.

In the early stages of recovery—before we've deposited enough "I love you's"—the thing to do if we relapse is to stop and recognize that what we're doing is trying to feed our lovesickness. Rather than get on our own case, we should just stop the destructive behavior and, instead, begin bombarding ourselves with "I love you's."

Love yourself anyway; fake it until you make it. Give yourself "I love you's" until you really believe that you don't deserve to hate yourself because you screwed up, that you can love yourself even if you relapse.

The payoff is that loving and forgiving yourself is the quickest way to end the relapse, the quickest way to get back on track. And it's the surest way to prevent relapse in the future.

It's important to remember that all of the addictive patterns we get into, all of the manifestations of lovesickness, are designed either to create an illusion of being loved and lovable, to blot out the feeling of not having enough love or to punish ourselves because that's what we deserve.

In all of those cases, criticizing and attacking ourselves only feeds and nourishes whatever behavior it is that we're trying to stop. Love yourself anyway, and do it abundantly.

Love Those Flaws!

If we were to divide self-love into grade levels, this would be graduate school. I encourage you to try it as soon as you can. We all do things that we hate, that we feel embarrassed and ashamed about. We hide these things from the world and even from ourselves when we can. We believe these things make us unlovable and unworthy of love.

These are the things that need to be loved the most.

Whether it's compulsive overeating or procrastination or lying or whatever, there's something within us that generates the behavior. Despising ourselves for these unattractive behaviors hasn't eliminated them, has it? If we looked closely enough, we would see that beneath all of these behaviors is the desire for love. *It doesn't make any sense to attack ourselves for doing things that are ultimately designed to get love.* Why not try loving yourself, anyway? And especially loving that part of you that generates all that crappy behavior.

In the South, where I went to undergraduate school, they have an expression, "Love the sinner, but not the sin." Carl Rodgers, a wonderful psychologist, said human beings need to be loved unconditionally even if their behaviors are unacceptable. We're not loving ourselves because we've lied or because we've relapsed or because we ate 17 Twinkies. We're loving ourselves because that sad, frightened little child within that's responsible for all those manipulative, embarrassing, annoying behaviors needs it.

CHAPTER 7

Treating Yourself With Unconditional Love

Here's a fascinating mind experiment created by Ron Smothermon: Who are you? What do you consist of? What things, what traits, what qualities go to make up who you are and what you are? Imagine you're putting all these things into a giant, clear plastic bag so you can easily see them. In first will go your physical being (your face, body, etc.), then your name, your color, race, religion, the place you live, your country of allegiance, all your clothes, everything you own, your beliefs, opinions, judgments and so on until everything is in there, including your mind, of course.

Now, let's take a look in the bag. Are you looking? If you forgot to include anything you think you are, go ahead and put it in. Great! Examine it all carefully.

But wait a minute. Do you get the feeling there's someone looking over your shoulder? Yeah, me too.

We're not the only ones looking at us, are we?

It's as if there were an Olympic committee inside us, closely observing us and keeping score. From time to time this committee holds up cards with numbers: 7.5, 7, 7.5, 8, 5 (uh-oh), 6.5, 7. Not doing so hot, are we? Our performance, our behavior—they're being constantly judged.

What is this committee? Where did it come from? It's very familiar; it seems to have been there all our lives. In fact, committee members began taking their seats in the judges' box when we were very young, long before we knew what was going on. While we were busy trying to "go potty," the Olympic committee was organizing (Smotherman 1980).

Today we call that committee our conscience. Our parents, brothers and sisters, uncles and cousins, school teachers and coaches, classmates and clergy—past and present—all of them have seats on the committee, in the arena of our minds.

It might not be so bad if they were minding their own business, but they're not. They're minding ours. Though we may protest the presence of these judges and the way they keep holding up score cards on everything we do, we may as well accept the fact that they are there. Our protestations only make them chuckle and smirk. They can't go away. We put them there. Each of us creates our own internal committee—our sense of right and wrong and our values—out of the world we grow up in and out of the people who help to shape us.

What can we can do to take advantage of this phenomenon? Since there is no avoiding the committee, we may as well make it work for us by convincing it to be on our side. Since the committee is always judging our performance, then let's really perform. Let's put on a great show!

This means treating ourselves with love. There are two general reasons for doing this:

1. If our internal judges see us abusing and mistreating ourselves, then they will conclude that this is the kind of treatment we deserve. They will be on the lookout for other opportunities to provide us with more pain and suffering. We'll sabotage ourselves; we'll become accident and incident prone. On the other hand, if we are treating ourselves with love, the observers will assume that we must be worthy of

kind treatment. They will then assist us, unconsciously, in experiencing more positive events.

2. As we nurture and take care of ourselves, we're going to just plain feel better. If we do the kinds of things that are positive and self-affirming, we're going to be healthier and feel more safe and secure.

Reverse The Roles

For the person to whom self-love is difficult or awkward, it may be hard to figure how to begin. How do you treat your *self* with unconditional love?

Here's a simple strategy which has profound implications: treat yourself *as if* you were someone you loved. Whenever you are faced with a dilemma, a situation you're not sure how to handle, ask yourself: "If someone I loved was in this situation, what would I want them to do?"

Suppose you are a newly sober alcoholic. You've just received an invitation to the wedding of your nephew. Now you know for sure, without an iota of a doubt, that there's going to be plenty of booze flowing. Champagne corks will be popping, toasts will be continuous, and everybody will be expecting you to drink up. Heck, there's going to be an open bar. An open bar!!!

So here you are, only a few weeks after your last drink, with an open invitation to get thoroughly polluted.

If you go to the wedding, there's a great risk that you'll relapse. At the least, you'll be absolutely miserable watching everyone drink. If you don't go, your nephew (whom you adore) will be hurt and the rest of the family will wonder what's wrong with you for not attending. Your nonattendance could set off a family feud that would last for seven generations.

This is a common scenario in which role-reversal is a healthy alternative:

First, instead of only three months of sobriety, imagine that you've got 30 years of sobriety. Not only that, but with those 30 years, you have also accumulated maturity and wisdom. Now that you're wise and stable, imagine that it's not you with the dilemma. Instead, imagine that someone you love very much—maybe a son or daughter—is now in your exact situation. This son or daughter whom you love so dearly has come to you to get advice. What would you want them to do?

The amazing thing is that people can usually see what others should do much better than what they themselves should do. We can give excellent advice to other people; advice that we'd never think of for ourselves.

Using this strategy of figuring out what we'd want a loved one to do if they were in our situation helps us get some objectivity. It introduces a loving perspective.

Because our love for ourselves is limited or perhaps nonexistent, we tend to give ourselves bad advice. If we are really down on ourselves, we will more often than not make the dumber, self-destructive choice. This has nothing to do with intelligence. Bright people can be even more self-destructive than others.

By switching seats with someone we love, however, we can access a wisdom we possessed all along. We did not really look for it because we have been out to sabotage ourselves.

If a person is attempting to deal with a particular destructive passion: gambling, sexual addiction, whatever, the simple question he or she should ask is, "What would I do if I loved myself?"

You don't give poison to someone you love. You don't send a compulsive gambler to the casinos. You don't send a sex addict to a massage parlor. But addicts take themselves back into their old dangerous haunts time and time again simply because they don't love themselves.

With practice, we can remind ourselves to ask this question whenever we're faced with a dilemma: "What would I do if someone I loved was in this situation?"

Do It For Yourself

A somewhat more direct strategy is to treat yourself as if you were someone you loved.

In my own early recovery, I was working full time, going

to school full time and going to 12-Step meetings in between. While this was going on, one of the things that suffered was my apartment. I had four cats at the time and they were leaving fur all over the apartment. You could just about trip over all the debris. It was like in the old Wild West movies, except instead of tumbleweeds in the street there were furballs blowing through my living room.

As if that weren't enough, in addition to the cat lint there were journal articles cascading off the desk, clothes lying around and coffee mugs everywhere. The place was a mess.

Now it turns out there was a young woman I was particularly fond of who was going to come over to my apartment for the first time. Naturally, I was concerned about what kind of impression I would make on her, so I had to deal with the clutter of my apartment.

I found a neighbor who had a vacuum cleaner and I got some boxes. Somehow I found the energy and time to pack up all these journal articles. I unearthed dirty clothes that had been stuffed under chairs developing new life forms. I did a good hour and one-half of cleaning, and at least got the surface grunge locked up and put away.

And as I was doing it, it occurred to me, "Geez, I come to visit myself every day. *Why not do this for me?* Why am I only interested in impressing this young woman? Why don't I do it for myself as well?"

So often we do things only because we're concerned about other people's approval. Are you more inclined to get it together when someone else is visiting than when *you* are?

Why not shift the focus to winning your own approval? Take the time to do things for yourself. Do you feel better when your house is clean?

Each of us has specific circumstances in which we can begin treating ourselves better and acting as if we loved ourselves.

Put The Shovel Down

The most obvious step is to begin abstaining from destructive or addictive behavior patterns. If you smoke, quit smoking. If you are in an unhealthy, going-nowhere relationship, get out of it.

Question: What's the first thing you must do to get out of a hole?

Answer: Stop digging.

When any addictive, destructive behavior pattern is taken on and confronted as an act of self-love, recovery becomes immeasurably easier. Indeed, one of the keys to successful recovery is doing it for yourself. When done with love, abstinence becomes not a sacrifice but a gift to oneself.

Take Care Of Your Body

One of the keys to self-love is demonstrating care and respect for your body. The things that your gym teacher told you all those years ago about proper nutrition, diet and exercise—guess what?—the teacher was right. The food we eat affects our mood, and our physical fitness dramatically affects our energy level and mental health.

Let's consider our relationship to food first. We can express self-hate, self-denial or self-love simply by selecting one food over another. While it seems so obvious and simple, it is incredibly difficult for many people to eat in a healthy manner.

We're so conditioned by convenience, by advertising and by what's on sale that we often don't take the time to step back and say: "What do *I* really like? What do *I* really enjoy? What tastes good to me? How much of it do I need?"

Pick The Foods That Make You Feel Good

It came as a shock to me when I discovered how completely brainwashed I am when it comes to food. For the longest time I thought that sugar, chocolate, caffeine and white flour were the four main food groups. For a while I had a thing for Wing Dings: a wholly artificial, reconstituted, socially unredeemable, could-have-been-made-by-Dow-Chemical-Corporation nonfood. I'd buy 'em by the box and freeze them, not because I was afraid they'd go bad—they already were bad. They probably had a shelf life into the year 2000. I froze them so that it would be more of a hassle to get to them, so I wouldn't scarf down a box in one day.

Now why did I crave this nonfood so badly? Well, sure.

there was some semblance of the taste of chocolate, but there were plenty of other foods that came closer to that taste. Like *real* chocolate, for example.

As embarassing as it is for me to admit it, I think I had a passion for Wing Dings because I was never allowed to have them as a child. Gosh, I hate being such a cliché, but there it is. I wasn't eating food. I was eating a resentment and trying to make up for lost time.

It takes just a little time and a little work to figure out what it is that *you* like to eat. The key is to see what makes *you* feel good and what your body (as opposed to what your 8-year-old repressed inner child) wants. Look at the food you're eating. Read the label. Is it worthy of you? Should this food be on your plate or on your ceiling (as ceiling tiles)? In other words, wake up!

Eat Lovingly

While I'm nagging about food, I may as well add the following. It's been estimated that as many as 70 percent of all alcoholics and probably a large percentage of other addicted individuals are hypoglycemic. This means that their body's reaction to sugar is out of balance and the insulin reaction is exaggerated after sugar is introduced into the body.

The result is that there's an initial energy charge followed by a crash, which may produce feelings of depression, anxiety, irritability, fatigue and even the shakes.

One of the things we all need to do is honestly look at how we react to things like sugar and white flour. Do we nod out a half hour after having sweets and does it make us depressed and irritable? Are we willing to trade off five minutes of pleasure for two hours or more of discomfort and confusion and lethargy?

Conduct an experiment. See how you feel if you eat a more healthy diet. Most nutritionists suggest switching to a low-fat, low-sugar diet with lots of fruits, vegetables and grains. Just see if doing so makes you feel better.

Although sugar and white flour have proven to be culprits for many people, there are others. Coffee and chocolate, because of their caffeine content, can be a source of some very bizarre, self-destructive behavior in some people. The point is: If you are what you eat, then eat those things that make you feel as good as possible.

What foods knock you out? What foods give you energy? Do you have a medical condition that calls for the reduction of fats or cholesterol? What's the most loving thing you can do at each meal?

Eat With Reverence

Another way to change your relationship with food, now that you've selected healthy ones, is to take a moment to bless your food before you begin eating. Whether it's a prayer that you learned as a child or a meditation you've created for yourself, look at the food and recognize that it is what your body is made of. Every cell of your body is constructed from the food that you eat. Your body and your brain are created from nothing but the food that you put into yourself.

Set aside a quiet moment to actually look at the food you are about to eat. Make it a conscious process rather than unconsciously inhaling everything that's edible.

As part of the hunting ritual, native Americans would bless the animal they killed. They would thank the earth for providing sustenance and thank the animal for giving up its life to sustain their own.

Take time to add sacredness to eating. This suggestion goes double for people who have an eating disorder of any kind (about 25% of our population). Take a moment, bless the food and appreciate it.

Many of us don't even taste more than the first bite of a meal. Even when we've paid a great deal of money to eat at a fine resturant, we just start in without paying any attention at all.

If you pay attention, you might find it harder to eat foods that are bad for you. If you realize that certain foods aren't good for you, you might make healthier, better choices. Junk foods might become less appetizing and healthier foods more appetizing.

Healthy Body, Healthy Mind

"Oh man. What a drag. I guess you're gonna tell me to start doing push-ups and running along the highway and, and, and—I'm already exhausted!"

Proper care and maintenance of your body includes keeping trim, healthy and in good condition. Feelings of exhaustion and achiness as well as impaired body movement due to poor physical conditioning are signals of limitation and "dis-ability." You can't feel safe or strong within your body.

The level of physical activity appropriate for you depends on your current physical condition. Get some advice from a physical therapist or trained exercise expert and map out a plan to restore yourself to the best condition your body can enjoy. What has been said elsewhere applies here as well: experiment. See if working out several times a week changes your mood, lifts your spirits and makes it easier for you to find feelings of love welling up within yourself.

Easy does it, though! You can't be rehabilitated overnight. Slow but sure wins this race. There's no benefit in pushing yourself until you strain a muscle or throw your back. Easy does it—but do it!

You might link exercise and affirmations. As you're running on a treadmill or working out on a weight machine, say to yourself, "I love you, _______________," with each repetition. Awesome.

Time For Yourself

The only thing that we can never get back again is this second. Whoosh! Gone forever. Yet ironically, people seem to treat time as if it had no value at all. As if it were a limitless commodity. *Au contraire, mon cher.*

Check it out: There are 168 hours in a week, and if a person lives to the average life expectancy of 72, there's something like 26,280 days or 630,720 hours in a lifetime. I don't know about you, but these do not seem like very large numbers to me. Particularly when we factor in how many of those years and hours have already been chewed up. Not only that, but we're going to be sleeping through about a third of the remaining hours.

The clock is ticking. Awareness of the brevity of life can either make us panic or it can lead us to a greater appreciation of the sacredness of life.

What are you doing with your time? Are you using it in a way that's an expression of love to yourself? Are you using this gift of life in the way you want?

I'm not suggesting that you call your boss and quit so you can go off to the mountains and meditate for the rest of your days. But it is an option. Perhaps the best thing you can do, all things considered, is grind out 60 hours of hard labor every week at a job you hate. Maybe. But maybe not.

Most people never step back and consider the fact that it is their life. Are you doing with yours what you really want to? Wouldn't it be a pity to die before you ever lived?

Are there changes that you know you need to make but you keep putting off? "I'll deal with this later." Are you waiting for that indeterminate time when you'll finally "get around to it"?

Tick tock, tick tock. Your time is finite. Ask yourself, "Is this truly how I want to be spending my time? Is this, given all the realities of my life, the best thing for me to be doing? Is this the life I want?" Most people can't give an unqualified yes to these questions. If you can, you are among the select few. Congratulations. Most of us must consider the possibility that we are living with some unnecessary limitations or burdens.

An exercise that might help you clarify your priorities involves imagining that you are now at the end of your life here on earth. You will soon pass on. What things do you want to be absolutely sure to have experienced? What would you regret the most having not done? Interestingly, most of the greatest regrets in people's lives don't involve misdeeds, but rather missed deeds.

Seize the day—with love.

Call Time Out

Speaking of time, another act of self-love is remembering the Sabbath and keeping it holy. One of the commandments, one of those items to have made it into the top ten, was to

	Mon	Tue	Wed	Thu	Fri	Sat	Sun
Morning							
Afternoon							
Early evening							
Late evening							

take a day off. This tidbit of wisdom has held up for about 6,000 years, give or take a century or two. Perhaps we should heed it?

We need a break. Unfortunately, this has become incredibly difficult for many because of economic pressures, responsibilities to families, and work. Many people work full time, go to school, raise children and have other responsibilities.

You would think that out of 168 hours in a week surely we can find a few in which to be good to ourselves.

What many people do instead is race around in constant activity—going to work, picking up the kids, eating, shopping, doing the laundry, cooking, cleaning—stop! After a couple of days at this pace, the idea arises: I deserve a reward. Unfortunately, because this occurs on a subconscious level without much loving deliberation, the reward comes in the form of some destructive outlet. We take a short cut to fill the void and binge on whatever our drug of choice is: cake, cocaine or a fling with the wrong person.

Create a grid (see above) that divides your week into the seven days and divide each day into four or five segments.

Every week should have several solid chunks of time set aside to do what you want to do. You may want to plan how this time is spent—otherwise you might find yourself filling the empty time slots with less than totally satisfying activities. Worse yet, you may find other people filling your time slots. What do *you* want to do? What is the most self-loving way you can spend this time?

People who've been tightly controlled, with little free time feel guilty about taking time for themselves. If you are such a person, consider the possibility that you will be a better mother or father or a better partner if you take the time to nurture yourself. If you can't do it for yourself, then do it for them.

Don't Forget To Play

The cemeteries are filled with indispensible people. Strange that the world somehow manages to keep on turning without them.

How often we get caught in the trap of believing that we have no time to get away, that we can't afford it or that things would collapse if we took off for a week. Trust me on this one. You're not that important.

Is the real problem that we know how to work but don't really know how to play? For the compulsive gambler, vacations mean spending their free time gambling. For the compulsive shopper, vacation time is merely shopping in another town. The drug addict uses up his vacation time to getting stoned.

Consuming passions eat up a lot of time. When they are left behind, there is a tendency to fill the free time with constructive activity. This may be to compensate for time wasted in the past or because we don't know what else to do. Vacations and play are essential parts of caring for yourself.

There's an infinite world of possibilities out there. Here's a short list of a few of them:

- Aerobics
- Amusement parks
- Antiquing
- Aquariums
- Art exhibits
- Astronomy
- Auto day trips
- Auto racing
- Auto shows
- Ballet
- Baseball
- Basketball
- Beaches
- Bicycling
- Bird-watching
- Board games
- Boating
- Bowling
- Boxing
- Camping
- Canoeing
- Card games
- Chess
- Classical music
- Comedy clubs
- Computers
- Cooking
- Dancing
- Dining out
- Fishing
- Flea markets
- Folk dancing
- Football
- Gardening
- Golf
- Hiking
- Hi-tech audio
- Horseback riding
- Ice skating
- Jazz
- Jogging
- Kite flying
- Lectures
- Long walks
- Macramé
- Martial arts
- Model-making
- Modeling
- Motorcycling
- Movie watching
- Needlepoint
- Opera
- Painting
- Photography
- Picnics
- Ping-pong
- Playing music
- Poetry readings
- Politics
- Pool
- Racquetball
- Rock concerts
- Rockclimbing
- Rollerblading
- Sailing
- Scuba diving
- Sculpting
- Shopping
- Sightseeing
- Singing
- Skiing
- Skydiving
- Softball
- Stamp collecting
- Swimming
- Tennis
- Theater
- Video games
- Woodworking
- Working out
- Videomaking
- Volleyball
- Zoos/nature

Which of these appeal to you? Lovesick individuals repeat the same patterns of compulsive activity. To break out of that rut, diversify. Add a few twists to your life. Experiment. See what you like and what you're not so crazy about. Surprise yourself. Do something, several somethings that you wouldn't ordinarily do. Expand your horizons.

You are gonna die, you know. Dead, cold in the ground. Kaput! Let this fact liberate and enliven you. Be sure to live before it's all over.

How's Your Imagination?

Close your eyes. No wait! Not yet. Read these instructions first, *then* close your eyes.

Imagine that you've got a nice yellow lemon sitting on the table in front of you. Cut that lemon in half. Now squeeze the juice of both lemon halves into a drinking glass. After you've squeezed both to juicelessness, lift one of the squeezed lemon halves to your mouth and suck its pulp slowly. Now pick up the glass of lemon juice and begin taking small sips.

Go ahead. If you haven't already done it, close your eyes and cut, squeeze, suck and sip the lemon juice.

Did your mouth water? If it didn't, you've probably got either no salivary glands or no imagination. Why did your mouth pucker up and water? You had these physical reactions because you were sipping your imagination! Your mind produced physical changes in your body.

Throughout each and every day, you imagine various possibilities. I used to wake up thinking that the soreness in my neck was a malignant cancer. The cancer had already spread throughout my body. Because of my illness, I would no longer be able to work, which meant I was going to lose my house. My cats would have to be placed in an animal shelter. I hadn't had my first cup of coffee yet and already I was abandoned, homeless and about to fall over dead.

It is incredible how we terrorize ourselves with our imaginations. Our sicko fantasies can wear down our immune systems and make us vulnerable to illness and injury. The emerging field of psychoimmunology and behavioral medicine is accumulating evidence linking stress, imagery and physical health. You are what you think.

Guided visual imagery is a technique for introducing *positive,* healing images to our subconscious mind.

In the Resources section I have listed a few books that go into greater detail on guided imagery. But you really don't need to go to that expense. You've already got an imagination. The trick is to get it to focus on some positive, soothing scenes. Here are a couple that I've picked up along the way. Feel free to use them or modify them to suit you.

The Light Of God

Lying down on a bed or the floor, with your eyes closed, imagine your body surrounded by an incandescent, beyond-white light. Imagine that this light, like the halo depicted in sacred art around the world, is the Light of God. The brightest light you've ever seen. *Relax into the light* and *effortlessly* observe it washing over you. With each breath inhale this light. With each exhalation it becomes brighter.

Set some time aside, perhaps when you are drifting off to sleep, and notice the light forming. Recall any image you may have stored in your memory of bright light and allow yourself to be surrounded by this light. Again, as in meditation, the key is not to try too hard. Easy does it. Let go. Let go. Let go.

Imagine the light surrounding you and coursing through you. It is traveling through your bloodstream. It's traveling directly through you and penetrating every cell of your body. Lighting up each cell, bringing healing, rejuvenating, enlivening energy and health.

Try to be playful with your imagination. Fascinate, don't concentrate.

Your Special Place

Another effective image involves creating the perfect dwelling place to which you can retreat whenever you wish. With your eyes closed, think of a location such as a snow-capped mountain or a long, private beach or perhaps a cottage in a forest or a field. At this ideal setting, visualize your ideal dwelling. Whether it's a large castle with spires and crystal or a cozy Hobbit-like hole in the ground, allow your own imagination free reign.

In this most perfect of settings and most perfect of homes, know that there is absolute safety and security. There is complete peace and ease and serenity in this magical place.

Now enter your special dwelling. What does it look like inside? Are the floors made of old oak or sparkling marble? What's on the walls? How does the air smell? Are there any plants or trees inside? How about a waterfall? Remember, you are free to create any place you wish. Let your imagination run wild.

Now, find your favorite, most perfect chair. Maybe it's carved out of an ancient tree or maybe it is some scruffy old sofa. Imagine yourself sitting in this most perfect of settings. Let go and breathe. Allow yourself time to be at ease. Completely safe and secure and carefree. Nothing to do except bliss out.

Make Love To Yourself

People generate a lot of shame and self-hate around their sexuality. For some, it's because of what they've been told about their bodies. Subtly, and not so subtly, parents, teachers and the media have taught us to treat our sexuality in confusing and disturbing ways. Most of us have been brainwashed or, more accurately, "braindirtied."

Many have been victimized by individuals who, in most cases, have been victims of sexual abuse themselves. Experiences of sexual abuse can create powerful barriers to the enjoyment of sex. With proper help, the consequences of this abuse can be relieved. Individuals who've been harmed in this way may have trouble with discussions about their sexuality. They have taken on the shame that belongs to the person who victimized them.

Another reason for difficulty with sexuality is that most people don't like their bodies, or at least some feature of their bodies. Their breasts are too big or too small; their penis is too large, too small; their lips are too thick, too thin, and so on.

Sexual orientation is another source of shame and self-hate for many. Many homosexuals grew up believing that being gay or being a lesbian was deviant and sick. Despite growing evidence that people are born with or develop these differences very early in life, people learn to hate who they are because of what turns them on.

Well, this is not an area that's mendable just through simple reading of a paragraph or two. Nevertheless, to begin let's consider some facts:

Our bodies, if they are healthy, come equipped with sexual apparatus. Nature gave us these body parts for a reason. I would like to submit to you that they were not given to us so that we would hate ourselves about their functions.

Hate is a particularly inappropriate response considering that these body parts can be such a great source of joy and pleasure. Fact is, the survival of our species beyond the next 70 years absolutely and totally depends on our use of these body parts, and I would encourage our joyful and safe use of them.

For some people, sexual relations with another person is a source of shame, pain, embarrassment and humiliation. For some, masturbation is a cause of tremendous self-hate, guilt and shame. In either case, the goal is to learn to *love yourself*, and that doesn't mean just from the waist up.

When masturbating, people should truly make love to themselves. Many use pornography, read erotica, lean up against a vibrating washing machine or use some other device to stimulate themselves. To each his own. But the fact is that after sexual release many people experience a feeling of disgust.

Why Do You Feel Guilty?

If you feel guilty, take some time to step back and work out why you feel that way. Many cases go back to conditioning, to what you've been told by parents who were embarrassed about their own sexuality or by a society that correctly needs to censure certain behavior *in public*. The problem is that we take these injunctions about masturbation or sexually acting out in public into the privacy of the bedroom and wrongly apply them to ourselves.

God or nature made every part of you, so love every part of you and the functioning of every part of you. In the preceding chapter I suggested that you marry the mirror. Well, this is the honeymoon.

Whether the sex is with someone else or yourself, with someone of the opposite sex or same sex, slow down and take your time. Our new loving, respectful approach to food is also appropriate for sexuality. Invite God into it, bless it, savor it.

Is what you are doing healthy? Some people may invoke a standard of *normalcy* rather than health as their criteria for what is and isn't okay. If you read the works of Kinsey and other sex researchers, you'll discover that most people have pretty broad allowances for their own sexual practices (even if they feel guilty about these practices and don't allow others to do as they do).

Look at all the people walking down the street or in the shopping mall. Almost all of them are regularly engaging in sex of one type or another. Your parents had to. So did your grandfather. And of course, so does that minister who's ranting and raving about the sinfulness of this or that.

The fact is that there is a wide range of possible actions for sexual pleasure, release and enjoyment. Keep it safe and healthy. Be honest about it.

If what you're doing is safe, not harming yourself or someone else, then why not love yourself for what you do? It is hard for many people to be at peace about their sexuality. The degree to which it's difficult, however, is the degree to which they should devote energies to reconciling it. Do whatever you do with love. Think kindly toward yourself Be kind to your mind.

Engage in sex with love for yourself and your partner. If you are awash in feelings of guilt or shame, take time to work on loving yourself in other ways. This is an area where a healthy therapist can be of great assistance.

Erotica may be of some help. Ancient forms of erotic literature are a celebration of healthy sexuality. If we depart from our Western tradition for a second and consider some of the wall carvings, statues and paintings of the ancient Far East, we see many examples of joyous expressions of sexuality. The world's oldest work of art—the Venus of Willendorf—is little more than a 20,000-year-old chunk of porno. Oh yeah, the art historians may call it a "fertility object," but you know what it really was.

Much more could be said about *acting as if* you love yourself. It helps to look at what you do, how you spend your time, who you spend your time with, and everything else that you do. Then, to the degree that it is possible, gradually, *gently,* eliminate those activities and uses of your time that are negative or that in one way or another say to our deeper observing self (our Olympic committee) that we don't really like ourselves. Replace those negative actions by demonstrating and expressing a healthy self-love.

CHAPTER 8

Find A Loving Community

As I write this, it's the middle of autumn just outside of Philadelphia. The leaves are putting on quite a show, surrendering their green coats for red, rust, yellow or brown. What catches my attention, however, is a group of geese flying above me, presumably going south for vacation.

You've seen flights of geese soaring majestically overhead, the leader out front and the other geese angling back on either side, forming a perfect V.

Naturalists have come up with some interesting findings concerning the "V-formation" of geese. As it turns out, flying in a V-pattern produces a dynamic in the air current that dramatically eases their flight. Apparently, the flapping of the leader's wings creates an updraft for the next goose, and the flapping of the one behind the leader creates an updraft for the next and so on. Together, they produce almost 60 percent more power for their flight. This sharing of strength, this mutual support, is how geese can fly great distances together. Can the same be true for us?

In this chapter I want to explore the role of membership in a loving community and how it can be a reliable source of unconditional love.

The tendency to want to be part of a group or community is quite old and possibly inherent in being human. People have been joining groups since the dawn of history. We're tribal in nature. Humans have always depended on group membership as a survival strategy.

Today, when survival no longer depends on escaping the swift claws of a tiger or avoiding the thunderous rush of a woolly mammoth, humans still band together for mutual support and protection. There are hundreds of thousands of groups, ranging from civic organizations like the Rotarians and Lions to political organizations like the League of Women Voters and United We Stand. There are countless churches, garden clubs, social clubs, business alliances, sports clubs, professional organizations, hate-based groups, philanthropic groups, recovery groups, hobby clubs, therapy groups, and all kinds of health clubs. And don't forget the gang that meets at the neighborhood bar.

This herding instinct is something that's hardwired into human nature. Take a look at people wearing the hats and jerseys of their favorite sports teams. It's just another way to identify with and feel connected to some larger group, and it's all driven by our need to belong. But wearing the star quarterback's jersey isn't going to do it for lovesick individuals. Their needs for love and connectedness are a bit stronger than what can be met by an article of clothing.

Membership in esoteric groups has only limited value for most people, even those who don't feel a desperate need of love and belonging. Most groups tend to focus on a cause or specific activity, and therefore only coincidentally meet the emotional needs of their members. It's my guess, however, that people join any group out of loneliness and need for connectedness; the particular cause is secondary. Even in amateur sports, do people get involved for the pursuit of victory and a good workout? Or do they join for the camaraderie and sense of community?

Membership in many worthwhile groups may take us a little part of the distance, but few fill a spiritual void within ourselves and reduce our compulsions. To address those deeper, more profound psychological and emotional needs it may be necessary to become affiliated with a group that has unconditional love as a primary function and goal.

How can we find such groups? How would we know that a community we are part of is, or could become, such a group?

Signs Of A Loving Community

How Are The Weak Treated?

In determining whether a particular group is likely to be a source of unconditional love, the first thing to consider is how that group treats its weakest members. An unconditionally loving group goes out of its way to welcome the fragile, poor and unattractive newcomer to the group. How does a group treat those with no money and few abilities? Are such people valued and welcomed or ignored and shunned?

The kind of group that will meet our needs is one that seeks to protect and care for the vulnerable and weak as well as the rich and strong. That's what makes it unconditional. Members extend themselves to make the outcast feel welcome (and in doing so, help themselves). When you find a group that does this, even though there's no apparent benefit in it for them, it is a loving community.

Welcome Wagon

The second criterion is how they treat strangers. Are strangers welcomed warmly? Do members undertake to show newcomers the ropes? Are they welcomed and supported or left to cast about, isolated and uncertain of their acceptance?

Financial Focus

The third question is the group's attitude toward money. Most groups handle financial matters; there's rent to be paid, operating expenses and other financial necessities. The questions to ask are: How much emphasis is placed on money? Is the focus on service or buildings? If the group values people solely because of their financial status or contributions, look elsewhere. Any love you find there will be conditional.

Group Leadership

Groups that are unconditionally loving will have leaders who help the group to focus on these values. They may or may not be talking about love, but either through their discussions or actions—reaching out to the frail and needy—they will be emphasizing love. Do the group's leaders give of their time and attention freely, setting a standard for other members? Or is their concern what's in it for them?

Focus On Service

The group's attitude toward service is telling. A loving group will put a high priority on service to others. Service is a basic core value of an unconditionally loving group.

Is The Group Reliable?

We all need reliable sources of unconditional love. When group members are available to help, wherever and whenever, the group is a reliable source.

At this point, you have to be wondering if there are any such groups. Where does one find these loving communities, if they do exist?

Where Do You Find Them?

As you have probably guessed, there aren't a whole lot of groups like I've described. But they are out there. Moreover, it is possible, and perhaps necessary, to convert a group that you are already a member of rather than finding a new one to join.

The Unconditionally Loving Family

Let's start by looking at a group you're already a part of—your family.

Families have the potential to be a reliable source of unconditional love but, as a rule, most families fall short of meeting these standards.

Is there something inherent in family life that puts conditions on love? Must the child feel she is loved only if she behaves a certain way? Must parents feel they're loved only if the children's wishes are granted? The American family, and I dare say families in all other cultures, tend to love each other conditionally. All too often, love seems attached to a long string of conditions. It's natural for parents to hope that their children will do better than they did. But children who grow up feeling that performance is everything are likely to feel deprived of love, and that love depends on how well they do. In other words, that love is conditional, and therefore undependable.

However, families can work toward the goal of loving each other unconditionally by adopting and applying unconditional love as their guiding ethic.

Families can have this as their core value. This does not necessarily mean all sweetness and smiles. Unconditionally loving families, like any other families, face serious challenges and conflicts. Throughout their trials, however, the question which guides their actions is: "What's the healthiest, most caring thing I can do for myself and the other members of my family?"

It's not likely that any family will become totally, perfectly loving. No group can do it perfectly. Regrettably, there aren't a lot of healthy role models. We all draw upon our own families and thus the luck of the draw! We also tend to get too much input about family life from television and movies. Television is rampant with bizarre families, and none of them provide a realistic image of what a healthy family is.

Religious Communities

Religious groups often talk about being founded on the principles of love, fellowship and service to others. But many get wrapped up in other matters, such as politics, finance, larger buildings, bigger congregations and so on. These are issues that fail to serve the emotional needs of the members.

Some congregations do provide unconditional love for members because they make it a priority. They are faithful to the scripture that calls for them to care for each other, to love and to serve. When a group embraces these values, unconditional love pours forth. For this to happen, however, there must be strong traditions of love and service which prevent other interests from getting in the way or leading them down the conditional path.

Your particular church or synagogue may be falling short of this ideal, but you can work from within, in a loving way, to bring about the fulfillment of these values. Take a stand for them. These values are undoubtedly expressed in your holy writings, or scriptures. If enough members of the congregation struggle to see that these values are practiced, you'll soon find yourself a member of a loving community.

Indeed, by lovingly taking that stand and advocating for the transformation of your church or synagogue, you yourself will be transformed. Don't complain. Act! Participating and advocating rather than criticizing is one of the surest ways of becoming part of a loving community.

Outside of mainstream religious groups, many smaller groups have been springing up, embracing the principles of community, fellowship, service and unconditional love. Such groups can be quite vital and spirit-filled. It's important, however, to remember the signs of a loving community mentioned earlier.

If you find a small group to your liking, whether it's relatively new or has an ancient tradition, you may have a better chance of working from within to make it a loving community. Newer groups obviously are more likely to be amenable to change. They don't have 2,000 or 5,000 years of tradition behind them. Nowadays many organized religions are undergoing so much strife and change that often there is more of an openness to new ideas there, too.

12-Step Fellowships

In our quest for loving communities, we can't overlook the 12-Step fellowships. There are numerous variations of 12-Step fellowships around the country and in other parts of the world. The first and the best known is Alcoholics Anonymous (A.A.). This organization's beginnings offer an excellent example of how unconditional love can manifest itself in a group or community.

It began where an alcoholic named Bill Wilson was having one heck of a time getting sober. For many years he had tried to quit drinking on his own to no avail. He joined a temperance society, but it was a very religious group and many drunks, including Bill, couldn't stomach the preaching.

One day in 1935, he was in Akron, Ohio, on a business trip. He was alone, very thirsty and quite fearful that he was going to do what he had done so many times before under similar circumstances—get woefully drunk.

In his pain and desperation he got an idea which ultimately transformed him and millions of other people like him. The idea was this: If he could find another alcoholic to reach out to and help, together they could keep sober. He called around to several churches in Akron and spoke to the ministers, asking if there was a drunk among their congregants. Most of the ministers thought Bill was looking for someone who had already sobered up and was in a temperance society. No, he wanted an active drunk!

Finally one minister said, "Yeah, I've got a real bad case for you," and hooked him up with a surgeon named Bob Smith. Dr. Bob made it clear that he did not want to be preached to. He had heard from all the temperance speakers, drum-bangers and Bible-thumpers, and he couldn't tolerate any more.

Bill Wilson's response struck a resonant cord in Dr. Bob: "Listen, I'm not here to help you," Bill said. "I'm here to help me." He suggested that between them they could help each other. That put an entirely different twist on it because now there were two drunks who could understand each other and, by sharing their understanding, help each other. They weren't asking anything of each other but love and support. They gave freely to each other. In that act, unconditional love was manifested.

Carved into the traditions of the 12-Step fellowships is the saying: "To keep it, you've got to give it away." One of the books written about Alcoholics Anonymous is called *Pass It*

On, based on the premise that the help each member received in getting sober had to be passed on to any newcomer who wanted help, with no dues, no fees and no qualifications except one: the desire to stop drinking (Alcoholics Anonymous World Services, Inc. Staff 1984).

Since that time, in addition to Alcoholics Anonymous' approximately 1.5 million members, other 12-Step groups have been formed. Narcotics Anonymous, Gamblers Anonymous, Sex and Love Addicts Anonymous, Overeaters Anonymous, Cocaine Anonymous, Smokers Anonymous, Debtors Anonymous, Co-dependence Anonymous and numerous others have adopted the same basic 12 Steps.

In addition, there are similar support groups for the family members and loved ones. For Alcoholics Anonymous, there's Alanon and Alateen; for Narcotics Anonymous, there's Naranon and so on.

Because A.A. has been around the longest, and because it is undeviating in its purpose, it is the largest recovery group. In 1993, A.A. had 89,000 groups in 141 countries. In recent years there has been a tremendous proliferation of the other 12-Step fellowships. It's been estimated that there are as many as 2 million members of 12-Step fellowships (of one kind or another) in the United States. If it were a religion—which it is not—that would make the 12-Step recovery movement one of the largest organized religions in America. It is clear, at least to those millions who belong to them, that these fellowships fill an important need.

Visit An Open A.A. Meeting

Anything I can say about 12-Step fellowships, anything that you can possibly learn from reading about them, can only give you the sketchiest idea about how these groups actually operate. One picture is worth a thousand words and one meeting is worth a thousand books. The best thing that you can do is pick up the phone and ask the operator for the number of one that interests you. Let's say it's A.A.

An A.A. phone number is listed in almost any town in America. Call it and ask for the time and address of an *open* meeting. Anyone may go to an open meeting. You can go to any closed meeting, too, if you have a desire to stop drinking, but the open meetings are available for people who aren't working on a particular issue and just want to learn about 12-Step fellowships and how they operate.

If the group is a healthy group and is functioning according to their traditions, you'll be warmly welcomed when you show up. By the way, they probably won't believe for a second that you don't have a drinking problem. Chances are good that they'll give you their phone numbers and tell you to keep coming back.

How do these fellowships operate? What are some principles that they use? A list of the 12 Steps and the 12 Traditions can be found in *Alcoholics Anonymous,* also referred to as the Big Book of A.A., available from Alcoholics Anonymous World Services, Inc. In the Resources section of this book I've listed sellers of 12-Step fellowship literature and identified other authors who have written beautifully about the 12 Steps, the 12 Traditions and these fellowships.

Since I have attended many different open meetings of these 12-Step fellowships, I'll describe what I've observed to give you some idea of what to expect.

At the beginning of most meetings, they'll ask if anyone's there for the first time. They do this because they want to welcome newcomers and let everyone know they're welcome. Newcomers don't have to identify themselves or say anything, but if they do they will be greeted warmly. Newcomers are usually given phone numbers of other members, a meeting list, and A.A. literature. Members will listen to newcomers and try to see if they have any practical needs they can help with. In every way they make it clear to newcomers that they're welcome and should keep coming back.

Members stress to newcomers that they are not alone, and that there are others with the same or worse problems. I remember at one of the first meetings I ever went to, there was a man who was horribly burned with severe facial scars. I later found out it was the result of drinking and smoking in bed, passing out and setting his bed on fire. With third-degree burns over most of his body, he was terribly disfigured.

But he was sort of the cornerstone of that particular A.A. group. He sponsored others and was loved by many. He had found a place where people saw his disfigurement not as a handicap but as a symbol of the disease and its consequences, as well as a triumph over that disease.

The point here is something I've seen time and time again at 12-Step fellowships: the strong reaching out to help the weak. It's a marvelous thing to witness.

Another notable phenomenon is the handling of "failure" by 12-Step fellowships, that is, what they do when a member relapses or, worse yet, when a member never seems to be able to "get it." I've seen people come into A.A. or N.A. meetings intoxicated. I've seen people roll in and out of the fellowship 10, 20, 30 times or more. In every case, they are welcomed back. They never give up on anyone. There's a 12-Step Tradition that plainly states: "The only requirement for membership is a desire to stop drinking." As long as he wants to quit, he belongs. He doesn't have to be sober.

There is tolerance for members who are obnoxious and defiant. By common consent the group generally responds with kindness, as if to say in one large communal voice, "We love you anyway."

In open A.A. meetings, N.A. meetings and other open 12-Step fellowship meetings, I've heard people say that the group loved them until they were able to love themselves. "You saw something in me that I couldn't possibly see. You loved me anyway, regardless of what I did." This is a very common experience and it embodies the magic of unconditional love.

In welcoming newcomers, some 12-Step groups will offer them temporary sponsors—individuals who have been sober and active members for years and who are available as a "big brother" or "big sister" (men help men, women help women). Lists of available sponsors are passed around at many meetings and available sponsors are often identified at meetings to let the newcomer know there's an experienced friend available just for the asking and without charge.

Keep Coming Back

Each 12-Step group has a specific purpose: recovery. Whatever an individual's problem is—alcoholism, drug addiction, sexual addiction, gambling addiction—each person there has reached the point of desperation. The group exists to help its members succeed, but if you don't succeed, that's okay. The rest of the world may tell you, "If you don't succeed, you're a failure," but you're never a failure in the eyes of a 12-Step group. They just ask you to keep coming back. The fellowship will always be there for you.

The group roots for its members who slip but who continue trying. It wants them to make it and will extend itself to any degree possible to help them do so.

No Leaders

Earlier I suggested that groups need leaders who are able to keep the focus on unconditional love as a core value. In the 12-Step fellowships, there are no leaders! One of the traditions is that a 12-Step fellowship meeting should never be organized. There's no hierarchy; power does not flow from the top down, because there is no top. The power of the group starts with the newcomer, flowing from the bottom up. Frequently, someone at a meeting will say, "The most important person at this meeting is the newcomer."

Although 12-Step groups are not organized in the traditional sense, there is a service structure that rotates freely. Anyone can chair a meeting, either by volunteering or being asked. The chairperson simply opens the meeting, states its purpose, usually asks members to read passages from the literature and introduces a speaker or a topic for discussion. The chairperson has no other authority. Periodically, there'll be a business meeting at which all members are welcome to decide how the money collected by passing a basket is used. Some of it goes to buy coffee, some to support the telephone answering service, some to subsidize publications.

"If It Ain't Broke . . . "

Twelve-Step groups are all based, as Scott Peck has said, on brokenness. If it wasn't broken, it wouldn't need fixing. And fixing is what they specialize in. "Each group has but one primary purpose—to carry its message to the alcoholic who still suffers." This is the 5th Tradition of Alcoholics Anonymous.

In a 12-Step fellowship, the focus is on honesty and self-disclosure. Everyone has personal problems, but most people don't like to talk about them for fear of being thought weak or vulnerable. In 12-Step fellowships, people are encouraged to talk about their problems. People *sharing* honestly about their pain and their fears, or their embarrassment over something that has happened, help themselves as they help the rest of the group. Rather than being a cause for ridicule or humiliation, open disclosure of one's insecurities or "weaknesses" becomes a means of generating love, acceptance and bonding.

It's the bond of participation in a common struggle. When one person talks honestly about a personal struggle, everyone else in the group is able to identify because it is likely that they've had the same struggle.

Like the geese flying in V-formation, the person who speaks honestly about his life lifts both himself and everyone else. Because in 12-Step fellowship there is no shame attached to what is said, others in the group feel they too can take a risk and open up. Invariably, they are greeted with love and acceptance. It's okay to feel vulnerable and weak; admitting that you're not okay is not unusual for both newcomers and oldtimers. In fact it's a source of a greater strength, both for veteran members and newcomers.

Willingness to *not* look good, willingness to show vulnerability in public through self-disclosure is incredibly liberating and empowering, not just to the one who does it but to others.

Another expression heard at 12-Step meetings: "You're only as sick as your secrets." People naturally tend to hide within themselves things that they're ashamed of. But those secrets fester and rot—unless they're exposed to the light of day. In a healthy 12-Step group, there's a sense of safety which encourages gut-level honesty.

Learning Through Osmosis

In a 12-Step group, no one says you must do this or that. You aren't required to tell any secrets, for instance. That's entirely up to you.

If you go to enough meetings, though, you hear others tell their stories and you often hear them telling *your* story. This gives secret-keepers the courage to open up and take their own risks. And people in a 12-Step meeting find themselves drawn closer to, not repulsed by, the one who opens up. Self-disclosure does not show that these people are weak, or evil or can't measure up; it shows only that they are human. When people get the courage to talk about their secrets, they find that it brings healing.

Listen Closely

One of the simplest ways of demonstrating our love for people is to listen to them. Our undivided attention is one of the most precious things we can give to another human being. How much more potent is it when 20 people, 30 people or even a hundred are listening to you?

After telling your story at a meeting, in some groups it's customary for the listeners to comment. But they seldom comment on the story of the one who has just spoken. Instead, they talk about themselves and how they may have handled, or mishandled, similar problems. Again, the same process is observed; one person speaks, everyone else listens.

One of the more odd phenomena is the absence of what some call "cross talk." It is extraordinarily rare to hear any member tell another member what they should or should not do. Instead, people talk about what they did when they were in a similar situation. This absence of "shoulding" on people creates freedom and ease. To the uninitiated, this lack of advice-giving appears cruel or at least indifferent. Actually, 12-Step groups have found that speaking about one's own experience is much better than giving advice.

They're Not Perfect

With all these glowing words about 12-Step fellowships, it's important to note that some groups are more loving and more sensitive to newcomers than others. If you should decide to get involved in a 12-Step fellowship, you won't necessarily find a group that fits your needs at first try. So shop around. Remember, each group is a community of individuals who are working on severe emotional problems, and members are at various stages of recovery. It's quite possible to wander into one meeting that is operating on a very high and evolved level and the next day walk into another meeting that seems to have a gray cloud hanging over it. For best results, try lots of meetings and go frequently.

Although people need to be part of a group, many people avoid group membership. This is particularly true among lovesick people who have a strong need of acceptance but an equally strong fear of rejection. As a result, people who go to their first few meetings often reject the group to avoid the possibility of being rejected. They figure the best defense is a good offense.

I've heard literally hundreds of people in desperate need of a loving fellowship say things like this: "Well, I'm not a joiner. I really don't like groups. I'm uneasy around lots of other people."

Lovesick people still want to find one other individual, one special person, who's going to heal all their pain, meet all their needs, fill all their voids. One person just can't do that. A 12-Step fellowship probably can't do it either, but it does have plenty of love to go around. One's emotional needs can be spread across a group with dozens of loving members. There's always an abundance of people with interest to share. If one person doesn't have exactly what's needed, others are able to pick up the slack.

Go With Someone Else

It's a good idea to go to your first 12-Step meetings with someone who is already a member. Going to one's first meeting alone is like going to a party where everybody but you seems to know each other. They're having a good time, enjoying themselves and you don't know a single soul. You'll feel more at ease going with someone you know.

Another suggestion is to go early. Most newcomers to a 12-Step fellowship try to arrive exactly at starting time. It's much better if you're the first to arrive; now everyone else who shows up is coming to your party!

Go to meetings that are in neighborhoods where you feel most comfortable. If you're gay, and you feel more comfortable around people of the same sexual orientation, there are gay meetings. There are meetings for women and for men, for lawyers and for doctors. There are meetings in the wealthiest neighborhoods and in the poorest neighborhoods. There are smoking meetings and nonsmoking meetings.

Finding Your Fellowship

Suppose you're not a compulsive overeater, an alcoholic or a drug addict. You don't gamble or do anything else terribly self-destructive or socially unacceptable. But you do have lovesick symptoms and you are looking for an unconditionally loving community. Where do you fit in?

As noted before, there's an enormous variety of 12-Step oriented fellowships that have sprung up around the country. One may very well be ideally suited to you. In the back of this book a list of telephone numbers for various 12-Step groups is provided. Your local telephone directory will list the numbers of the groups operating in your area. Once you begin to attend, you'll find out about other groups. Give it a try: it's a great adventure.

You can also start your own group. It doesn't even have to be 12-Step oriented. New groups are forming all the time, in addition to those existing groups which might fill the bill. People are social—especially those people that call themselves loners. Find a group that you feel comfortable being a part of, one that can love you.

CHAPTER 9

TAKE TWO PUPPIES AND CALL ME IN THE MORNING

Although "pet therapy" has been employed in some form since the late 1700s, the formal prescription of other species as healers is a relatively recent practice. Over the past decade, several reports have documented the therapeutic value of pets. Epileptics, prison inmates, people with high blood pressure, emotionally disturbed children and the institutionalized elderly have all shown marked improvement under the care and influence of pets.

In one experiment, volunteers either petted their own dogs or a dog with whom they were unfamiliar while researchers monitored the volunteer's blood pressure. The researchers found that subjects who petted their own dog experienced significantly greater decreases in both systolic and diastolic blood pressure than when they petted a strange, yet otherwise friendly dog. The researchers concluded that petting an animal with whom "bonding" or attachment had developed produces a measurable calming effect that might benefit individuals suffering from high blood pressure.

In another study, patients who were about to undergo dental surgery were given either hypnosis or told to observe the tropical fish in their dentist's office aquarium. The researchers found that contemplation of the fish tank led to significantly greater patient comfort than hypnosis. The dentist/researchers also reported that the fish gazers were more cooperative and generally better patients than those who were given hypnosis.

A University of Pennsylvania researcher who surveyed more than 800 cat owners found that 99 percent considered their cats to be a member of their family, 89 percent allowed their cat to sleep on their bed, 92 percent claimed that their cat was aware of their moods, and 58 percent reported that they talked to their cats about important matters at least once a month!

Because there is so little research concerning the therapeutic value of pets and absolutely no research on the effect of pet ownership on the recovery process, I guess I'm free to say just about anything I want. In light of the *paw*city of research data, what follows are some thoughts and suggestions about the role which Snaggles, Tiberius and Waldo can play in helping people recover from lovesickness.

*Purr*haps most important is the fact that while people often place conditions on the love they give, pets do not. Dogs, for example, are extremely indiscriminate; most breeds love everybody! Dogs never seem to have bad days, get moody or become unfaithful. It's the way they are made. This makes them a cheap, reliable source of unconditional love.

Some hair-splitters may choose to quarrel about whether an animal is capable of being truly loving. The question of "true love," however, is irrelevant. What I feel when my cat, Tyro, runs up and sort of knocks into me sideways, rubbing her body against my shin so that I stumble and just about bust my nose, sure seems like love. Love that is given freely, consistently and with no strings attached. As one recovering friend said, "When I first got sober I was afraid of everybody, including the people in Alcoholics Anonymous. But funny as it may sound, I always knew that my dog didn't judge me. I could speak to my dog and he seemed to understand me. I don't know, but somehow he seemed to be the only one who did understand." Or as a client of mine once said, "The more I learn about people, the better I like my cat."

Have You Hugged Your Dog Today?

The need for close, nonsexual physical contact, or "contact comfort" is well established. To hold and be held; to feel the warm touch of another—this is a basic human need (Harlow 1971). Unfortunately, this is often hard to come by. Most of the touching we humans do is either accidental, violent or sexual. For the lovesick individual, the need for kind, nonsexual physical contact is especially strong. Although a fair amount of hugging goes on in the various 12-Step groups, for many such close human contact is often interpreted as a sexual advance (which it sometimes may be). This can be a source of anxiety for many a newcomer to A.A. But patting a dog on the head or holding a cat that is tolerant of such affection from a human can be a most comforting experience.

In a fascinating study conducted by two doctors at the University of Pennsylvania, the survival rates of 92 individuals who had been hospitalized after suffering a heart attack were compared. Although all individuals in the study were provided with proper medical care during the year after their attack, the survival rates of these individuals varied significantly. In an analysis of the findings, one factor that best predicted the likelihood of post-heart attack survival was pet ownership! Of the 53 people who owned pets, three (or 5.6 percent) died during the year following their heart attack. Of those who did not own pets, 11 of the 39 (or 28.2 percent) died within one year. Do pets help to heal broken hearts? Even the ones who've never gone to medical school seem to know what to do.

Cats and dogs are great entertainers. I never tire of watching my cats wrestling with each other. I even enjoy watching them take a catnap. Dogs tend to be more active performers. Dogs love to go for walks. Being walked by a dog is not just a source of excercise, it is also an excellent way of meeting people. Many a friendship between people was started only after their pooches first gave each other a good sniffing. Finally, there is no end to the types of tricks that a dog can be taught. (Unless you are a professional animal trainer, cats, alas, are pretty much a zero in the "tricks" department.) All of this low-cost entertainment may help to jump-start a sluggish endorphin system.

Pets can be ice-breakers. Please don't take me literally—pets should never be used to break ice, or even scrape the frost off windshields. Pets, however, can be an endless source of distraction and conversation. When a distant relative, new friend or even an in-law comes to visit, it can be tough starting a conversation. A socially conscious pet will sense that an awkward silence has descended upon a gathering and will come bounding into the den and show off his snappy "handshake" or "roll over" routine. Nothing like a good "sit-up" demonstration to prevent a dull evening.

There's nothing better than rescuing a stray from a shelter to combat feelings of worthlessness, guilt and shame which are so common in lovesickness. Although these feelings can be reduced by practicing the recommendations in this book, there's no doubt that an act of charity can help a person get over a poor self-image. Of all the potential good deeds that a person performs, saving the life of another certainly must top the list, even if it's the life of a pooch.

While opportunities to save the life of another person don't come along all that often, saving the life of a dog or a cat does. And the beauty of it is that it involves little more than a trip to the animal shelter. As is well known, most animals placed in shelters will only be maintained for a limited tim2e before they are put to sleep. When a cat or a dog is adopted from such a facility, a life has truly been saved (a fact of which I frequently remind my cats).

Pet Picking Pitfalls

More than half of all American households have at least one pet. Unfortunately, not everyone who has a pet is happy with it. After all, there are plenty of ways to go wrong in choosing a companion animal. In order to reduce the likelihood of a bad match, here are some guidelines that should be kept in mind when selecting a pet.

Time Commitment

When staring into the eyes of a puppy who's doing hard time at the local animal shelter, few people think to ask themselves this: "Do I have enough time to take proper care of this animal?" As a rule, dogs require far more time and attention than cats. If a dog is left alone for an extended period of time, the owner may return to find that her closets have been trashed and her rugs need to be incinerated. If you leave a typical cat alone, on the other hand, it will usually be grateful for the peace and quiet. Dogs need to be walked several times a day. Cats would find such an experience humiliating.

Expense

Contrary to what you might expect, the cost of owning an animal cannot be calculated by the pound. On the average, cats and dogs involve just about the same expense—approximately $500 per year. There is the cost of food, vaccinations and visits to the vet. Then, of course, there are visits to your local emergency room after you tried to help your vet give your cat its shots. Finally, there are all those unexpected expenses. One summer, for example, my cats decided to play host to a squadron of homicidal fleas. It ended up costing me over $200 in flea dips, sprays and "special" shampoos before the ordeal was over. The one benefit was tht I learned how to scratch myself with my hind leg.

Space Requirements

While cats are wonderful for individuals living in an apartment or a small house, dogs should only be considered if they are small enough to be bullied by the feline next door. In the wild, cats generally stake out a limited territory and are happiest when they stay within that area. Consequently, they do quite well in even very tiny apartments. Dogs need extra room for wagging their tails and fetching things.

Allergies

Before a pet is adopted and taken home, you should spend some time in the animal's presence to determine if you or members of your family have an allergic reaction. People tend to be allergic to cats more often than dogs. Discovering that you are allergic to an animal after you've become attached to it has kept many an allergist in business. Sometimes, even an allergist can't help. I remember the dilemma my parents had when they discovered that my brother was severely allergic to cats. I still miss my brother, but I know he's happier in his new home.

Psychopetology

It is important to consider the mental condition of the animal before taking it home. After all, at least *one* of you should be emotionally stable. Emotional disorders can often be detected in animals without the use of expensive psychiatrists, psychological tests or residential treatment programs.

The quickest test of an animal's mental condition is to simply observe how it reacts when you pet it or pick it up. If, upon being picked up, a cat transforms into a Steven King character and attempts to shred you like a government document, PUT THE CAT DOWN!. It probably doesn't like being held. Interestingly, though, cats that act like they're demonically possessed when held can otherwise be perfectly charming companions. If they purr when you pet them, or if they rub up against you or come to you when you say "Pssst, ya wanna go play with some mice?" then chances are good that you have a cat that is a people-lover. On the other hand, if the cat treats you like some sub-feline species—if it hisses and spits at you whenever you get close—you'll never be able to change its opinion. This can be devastating for the person who already feels unloved: "Even my cat will have nothing to do with me." Find out before you leave the shelter and save on mental health counseling.

Dogs evolved as highly social animals that run in packs and enjoy hanging out at Milkbone parties. Because of this, when a dog sees its first human it generally concludes that the human is just a pitifully deformed dog and feels sorry for him. That's why they're good at loving us unconditionally: they pity us. A word of caution, though: If a dog is fond of showing you that its teeth are bigger, sharper and whiter than yours, then it's best to leave that dog for Dracula.

Neither the most outgoing puppy in the litter nor the runt of the litter will be especially good candidates for learning tricks, balancing your checkbook or helping you find dates. Go for the middle-of-the-pack puppy. That cute tiniest one may be darling to look at now, but it will have adult puppy of a dysfunctional litter issues later. Remember: beauty is only fur deep.

A major consideration in selecting a dog is its breed. Studies have demonstrated that clear differences in temperament exist among the various breeds. In general, the most hyperactive dogs are terriers and schnauzers, while the bloodhound, basset hound and retrievers are the most laid back. The most easily trained animals are Dobermans, poodles and shepherds. Don't even try sending a basset hound, dachshund or Pekingese to puppy college—they'll never even make it to class. Spaniels, retrievers, poodles and collies get the highest scores for love and affection. For lovesick individuals, however, mongrel mutts may be the best of all.

Are You Ready?

One last issue that needs to be addressed concerns determining whether a person is ready to take on the responsibility of owning a pet.

If you're not doing a very good job of taking care of yourself, then adding a pet isn't going to make life any easier. Dogs usually take a *minimum* of 10-20 minutes a day (feeding, walking, brushing and counseling). Cats are infinitely easier to care for than dogs but they still need some attention on a near daily basis. Scooping the litter box is the cat owner's curse.

The best suggestion that could be offered to the individual who is pondering the question, "To pet or not to pet?" is to honestly examine how well they are fulfilling their current obligations.

If you are handling your life responsibly, then a pet may be a terrific way to add some love to your life. On the other hand, if you're not taking care of your own basic needs and think that maybe a little puppy is going to help you straighten out your life . . . oh brother. Don't do it. Practice with yourself first—be your own master! Once you've consistently taken care of yourself—that is, taken yourself for walks, kept fresh water in your water dish and brushed your fur on a regular basis—then you'll be ready for four-legged company.

RESOURCES

Cited In The Text

——. *Alcoholics Anonymous. 3d, rev. ed.* New York: Alcoholics Anonymous World Services, 1976.

Alcoholics Anonymous World Services, Inc. Staff. *Pass It on: The Story of Bill Wilson & How the A.A. Message Reached the World.* New York: Alcoholics Anonymous World Services, 1984.

Bradshaw, John. *Healing The Shame That Binds You.* Deerfield Beach, FL: Health Comunications, 1988.

Harlow, Harry. *Learning to Love.* New York: Ballantine, 1971.

Sadock, Benjamin J., Harold I. Kaplan and Alfred M. Freedman. *Comprehensive Textbook of Psychiatry.* Baltimore: Williams and Wilkins, 1985.

Peck, M. Scott. *Road Less Traveled.* New York: Simon and Schuster, 1980.

Smothermon, Ron. *Winning Through Enlightment. 6th ed.* San Francisco, California: Context Publications, 1980.

Steele, Stanton and Archie Brodsky. *Love & Addiction.* New York: Taplinger, 1975. *This book sheds great light on understanding addictive relationships.*

The following are books which I've enjoyed and found helpful. I've included some comments on each to provide additional guidance should you wish to pursue these topics futher.

Meditation

Easwaran, Eknath. *Meditation: A Simple Eight-Point Program for Translating Spiritual Ideals into Daily Life.* Tomales, California: Nilgiri Press, 1991. *A thorough eight-point meditation program is described, devoid of a lot of mumbo jumbo. A good book.*

Golas, Thaddeus. *The Lazy Man's Guide to Enlightenment.* New York: Bantam, 1972. *I guess this eighty-page book is one of my all time favorites. Every few years I pick it up and re-read it. He doesn't exactly describe any meditation techniques, but rather, a perspective for "lazy" seekers.*

Hanh, Thich Nhat. *The Miracle of Mindfullness.* Boston: Beacon Press, 1976. *A wonderful book offering excellent guidance on meditation.*

LeShan, Lawrence L. *How to Meditate: A Guide to Self-Discovery.* New York: Bantam Books, 1974. *A brief book describing a variety of meditation techniques.*

Levine, Stephen. *Guided Meditations: Explorations and Healings.* New York: Anchor Books, 1991. *A variety of useful meditations many of which are designed to help us through challenges such as chronic pain, loss or grief.*

Sujata. *Beginning to See.* San Francisco, California: Apple Pie Books, 1985. *This is my favorite meditation book; it's easy to read and has lots of neat illustrations.*

Suzuki, Shunryu. *Zen Mind, Beginner's Mind.* New York: Weatherhill, 1985. *Excellent information on Zen meditation.*

Yogananda, Paramhansa. *Metaphysical Meditations.* Los Angeles, California: Self-Realization Fellowship Publishing, 1976. *A great little book filled with various themes to meditate upon.*

Affirmations

Gawin, Shakti. *Living in the Light.* San Rafael, California: New World Library, 1986. *A radical expression of the mind/body connection and the transforming role of affirmation.*

Hay, Louise L. *You Can Heal Your Life.* Santa Monica, California: Hay House, 1987. *Louise has written a few books on affirmations; all have specific affirmations for specific occasions. I have friends that swear by them. For more info: 1-800-654-5126*

Holmes, Ernest Shurtleff. *This Thing Called You.* New York: Putnam & Sons, 1948. *Holmes, the founder of the new thought religion called Science of Mind (also known as Church of Religious Science) has published numerous books on the subject of affirmative prayer. Science of Mind also publishes a monthly magazine called* Science of Mind *which is a fantastic source of affirmations and information about spirituality. (1-800-382-6121).*

Mandino, Og. *The Greatest Miracle in the World.* New York: F. Fell, 1975. *A neat little book which ends with a great "Memo from God"; not exactly an affirmation but a wonderful message.*

Meditation/Affirmation & Healing

Borysenko, Joan. *Guilt is the Teacher, Love is the Lesson.* New York: Warner Books, 1990. *This book offers an integration of psychology and spirituality; many exercises are suggested.*

Cousins, Norman. *Head First: The Biology of Hope.* New York: E.P. Dutton, 1989. *This book summarizes the research literature on the relationship between the mind and the body; physical and mental health.*

Siegel, Bernie S. *Peace, Love & Healing.* New York: Harper & Row, 1989. *More on the relationship between body, mind and soul.*

Books About Addiction & Recovery

Mooney, Al, Arlene Eisenberg and Howard Eisenberg. *The Recovery Book.* New York: Workman Press, 1992. *A great book on recovery from addiction; also an excellent introduction to the 12 Step recovery movement.*

Support & Recovery Groups

There's a hundreds of "self help" groups to choose from. I've listed just a few. Occasionally groups change their telephone numbers; often times there are local groups which have numbers in your phone directory. In any case, the numbers provided below are most helpful when you haven't been able to track down a group using your local phone directory. I have provided a brief description in italics of some groups when their purpose is not obvious.

Most of these numbers come from an excellent book called ***The Self Help Sourcebook*** (Denville, New Jersey: New Jersey Self-Help Clearinghouse, Saint Clares-Riverside Medical Center, 1986) which can be purchased for about $10 from the New Jersey Self-Help Clearinghouse by calling (800) 367-6274. In addition to including hundreds of self-help groups, this book offers suggestions for starting your own group. They can also be contacted for information and referral to other groups which may not be listed here. *(Thanks Lynn Friedman for turning me on to this book.)*

Other national clearinghouses for support group information are:

American Self-Help Clearinghouse	201-625-7101
National Self-Help Clearinghouse	212-642-2944

12 Step Addictions-Oriented Groups

Alcoholics Anonymous	212-870-3400
Narcotics Anonymous	818-780-3951
Overeaters Anonymous	310-618-8835
Gamblers Anonymous	213-386-8789
Sex & Love Addicts Anonymous	617-332-1845
Sex Addicts Anoymous	612-339-0217
Nicotine Anonymous	415-922-8575
Codependence	602-277-7991
Debtors Anonymous	212-642-8222
Cocaine Anonymous	800-347-8998

For Family Fembers and Friends of Addicted Individuals

Adult Children of Alcoholics	310-534-1815
Al-Anon Family Group	800-356-9996
Alateen/Ala-preteen-Alatot	800-344-2666
Nar-Anon	310-547-5800
Gam-Anon	718-352-1671

Families Anonymous 800-736-9805

Addiction Support Groups for Special Groups

International Doctors in AA 314-781-1317
For physicians and psychologist in AA

International Nurses in AA 913-842-3893

International Pharmacists Anonymous 908-735-2789
Support for addicted/recovering pharmacists

Anesthetists in Recovery 612-724-8238

Social Workers Helping Social Workers 203-489-3808

Psychologists Helping Psychologists 313-278-1314

Rational Recovery Systems 916-621-4374
Non-spiritually based recovery support

Secular Organizations for Sobriety 716-834-2922
Non-spiritually based recovery support

Jewish Alcoholics, Chemically Dependents
& Significant Others 212-397-4197

Overcomers Outreach 213-697-3994
Christian ministry of self-help groups for various addictions

Intercongregational Alcoholism
Program 708-445-1400
For Roman Catholic women who are or who have been in religious orders and are recovering from chemical dependencies

Other Support Groups: Psychological Conditions

Depression After Delivery 800-944-4773

Depressives Anonymous 212-689-2600

National Depressives & Manic Depressives Association	800-82-NDMDA
Homeless and Missing Network	703-524-7600
National Alliance for Mentally Ill (NAMI)	800-950-NAMI
Siblings & Adult Children's Network *Support for family of mentally ill*	703-524-7600
Emotions Anonymous	612-647-9712
Emotional Health Anonymous	818-240-3215
International Association for Clear Thinking	800-236-8311
Neurotics Anonymous	501-221-2809
Recovery, Inc.	312-337-5661
Grow *12 Step support group for mental health recovery*	609-794-1033
Schizophrenics Anonymous	313-477-1988
Obsessive-Compulsives Anonymous	516-741-4901
Agoraphoria in Motion (AIM)	313-547-0400
Anxiety Disorders Association of America	301-231-9350
Phobics Anonymous	619-322-COPE

Family/Parenting Support Groups

Adoptees In Search *Adult adoptees in search of birth relatives*	301-656-8555

Adoptive Families of America	612-535-4829
Adoptee Liberty Movement Assn *Adult adoptees in search of birth relatives*	212-581-1568
North American Council on Adoptable Children	612-644-3036

Support groups for parents

National Foster Parent Association	713-467-1850
Association of Couples for Marriage Enrichment	919-724-1526
No Kidding	604-538-7736

Support for couples without children

WOOM (Wives of Older Men)	908-747-5586
Family Resource Coalition	312-341-0900
Grandparents as Parents (GAP)	310-983-6555
Mothers of Pre-Schoolers (MOPS)	303-420-6100
Tough Love International *Self-help for parents of difficult children*	800-333-1069
National Organization of Mothers of Twins	505-275-0955
Association for Children for Enforcement of Support	800-537-7072
Banana Splits *Support for children affected by divorce or parent's death*	800-359-0961
Joint Custody Association	310-475-5352

North American Conference of Separated & Divorced Catholics	401-943-7903
Parents Without Partners	800-637-7974
Single Parent Resource Center	212-947-0221
Batterers Anonymous *For men who are abusive*	714-355-1100
National Coalition Against Domestic Violence	800-333-SAFE
Believe the Children *For parents of children who have been victimized by someone outside of the immediate family*	310-379-3514
Parents Anonymous	800-421-0353
Incest Survivors Anonymous	310-428-5599
Survivors of Incest Anonymous	410-433-2365
Sexual Abuse Survivors Anonymous	313-882-9646
Stop Abuse by Counselors	206-243-2723
VOICES in Action *Adult victims of childhood sexual abuse*	800-7-VOICE

Sexuality/Gay & Lesbian Support Groups

Dignity *Gay and lesbian catholics*	800-877-8797
International Foundation for Gender Education *Support for cross-dressers & transexuals*	617-899-2212
National Gay & Lesbian Task Force	202-332-6483

Parents & Friends of Lesbians & Gays Federation	800-4-FAMILY
Prostitutes Anonymous *Support for people wishing to leave the sex business*	818-905-2188
Homosexuals Anonymous *A Christian support group for individuals wishing to live non-homosexual lives*	800-253-3000

Other Support Groups: Medical Conditions

Rainbows for All God's Children *Grief support groups*	708-310-1880
Compassionate Friends *Grief support when a child dies*	708-990-0010
Parents of Murdered Children	513-721-5683
SHARE: Pregnancy & Infant Loss Support	314-947-5000
Survivors of Suicide (SOS) *For families of suicide victims*	414-442-4638
AIM (Amputees in Action)	619-454-9300
Mutual Amputee Aid Foundation	818-509-3400
Parents of Amputee Children	201-731-3600 ext. 291
Autism Society of America	301-565-0433
American Council of the Blind	800-424-8666
National Federation of the Blind	410-659-9314

Council of Families with Visual Impairments	216-381-1822
Phoenix Society for Burn Survivors	800-888-2876
United Cerebral Palsy Association	800-872-1827
American Society for Deaf Children	800-942-ASDC (voice & TDD)
National Association of the Deaf	301-587-1789 (TTY); 301-587-1788 (voice)
National Fraternal Society of the Deaf	800-676-NFSD
Self-Help for Hard of Hearing People (SHHH)	301-657-2248 (voice); 301-657-2249 (TDD)
National Head Injury Foundation	800-444-NHIF
Attention Deficit Disorder Association	800-487-2282
Children with Attention Deficit Disorder	305-587-3700
Learning Disabilities Association of America	412-341-1515
The ARC *Support for retarded individuals and their families*	817-261-6003
National Downs Syndrome Congress *Parents support group*	800-232-NDSC
Association of Birth Defect Children *Support for families*	407-629-1466

Spinal Cord Society	218-739-5252
Hear Our Voices *Support for individuals with speech impairments*	216-262-4681
DisAbilities Anonymous	212-989-3416
Family Centered HIV Project	301-654-6549
Gay Men's Health Crisis *Support for those affected by HIV*	212-807-6655
HIVIES *12 Step group support for people with HIV*	708-724-3832
National Association of People with AIDS	202-898-0414
Alzheimer's Disease Association	800-272-3900
National Association for Sickle Cell Disease	800-421-8453
Rheumatoid Arthritis Self Helpers	502-581-1945
Bone Marrow Transplant Family Support	203-646-2836
AS-IS (American Silicone Implant Survivors)	314-821-0115
Breast Implant Information Foundation	714-830-2433
Candlelighters Childhood Cancer Foundation	800-366-2223
National Coalition for Cancer Survivorship	301-585-2616

Leukemia Family Support Foundation	800-284-4271
HEAL (Human Ecology Action League) *Support for persons affected by multiple chemical sensitivities*	404-248-1898
National Foundation for Chemically Hypersensitive	517-697-3989
National Chronic Fatigue Syndrome Association	816-931-4777
National Cleft Palate Association	412-481-1376
American Diabetes Association	800-232-3472
Juvenitle Diabetes Foundation	800-223-1138
Diabetes Anonymous *Information for starting your own group*	408-746-2022
American Anorexia/Bulima Association	212-734-1114
National Anorexic Aid Society	614-436-1112
National Association of Anorexia	708-831-3438
Endometriosis Association	800-992-3636
Epilepsy Foundation of America	301-459-3700
AboutFace *Support for individuals with facial disfigurement*	416-944-FACE
Let's Face It *Support for individuals with facial disfigurement*	508-371-3186

Fetal Alcohol Network	610-384-1133
Mended Hearts *Support for individuals affected by heart disease*	214-706-1442
National Hemophilia Foundation *Support for individuals affected by hemophilia*	800-42-HANDI
Herpes Resource Center	919-361-8488
Herpes Anonymous	516-334-5718
Impotents Anonymous & I-Anon	615-983-6064
Simon Foundation *Support for individuals affected by incontinence*	800-23-SIMON
IP Support Network	313-729-7912
Resolve *Support for infertile couples*	617-623-0744
American Association. of Kidney Patients	800-749-2257
American Liver Disease Foundation	800-223-0179
Lupus Foundation of America	800-558-0121
American Lupus Society	800-331-1802
Myasthenia Gravis Foundation	800-541-5454
American Narcolepsy Association	800-222-6085
Narcolepsy Network	914-834-2855
United Ostomy Association	800-826-0826

National Association to Advance Fat Acceptance	916-443-0303
Take Off Pounds Sensibly (TOPS)	800-932-8677
American Chronic Pain Association	916-632-0922
American Parkinson's Disease Association	800-223-2732
Parkinson Support Groups of America	301-937-1545
Parkinson's Education Program	800-344-7872
Courage Stroke Network	800-553-6321
Stroke Clubs	409-762-1022
Tourette's Syndrome Association	800-237-0717
National Black Women's HealthProject	800-ASK-BWHP
Little People of America	800-24-DWARF
International Foundation for Stutterers	609-275-3806
National Center for Stuttering	800-221-2483
National Stuttering Project	415-566-5324
Disabled American Veterans	606-441-7300
Vietnam Veterans of America	202-628-2700

Women's Support Groups

Business & Professional Women/USA	202-293-1100
Love N Addiction *Support groups based on the book:* ***Women Who Love Too Much***	203-423-2344
National Organization of Women (NOW)	202-331-0066

Miscellaneous Support Groups

Gray Panthers *Multigenerational advocacy group*	202-387-3111
Phenix Society *Holistic & spiritually-oriented fellowship*	203-387-6913
ARTS Anonymous *12 Step oriented support for artists seeking to fullfil creative potential*	212-969-0144
Parents of Murdered Children	513-721-5683
Cult Awareness Network	312-267-7777
Child Survivors of the Holocaust	310-657-6437
Messies Anonymous	305-271-8404
International Association for Near Death Studies	203-232-4825
Students Against Drunk Driving	508-481-3568
Toastmasters International *For those hesitant to speak in groups*	714-858-8255
Workaholics Anonymous	310-859-5804

Love Quotes

Over the years I have been collecting quotes which illuminate the distinction between love and lovesickness. I find it particularly instructive to note that confusion over the differences between these experiences is quite old. The reader will notice that most of these quotes are decidely negative about "love." It is important to remember that these quotes were selected to focus upon lovesickness, not healthy love.

Love And Intoxication

How much better is thy love than wine

—Song of Solomon, 4:10
Bible, Old Testament

Oh, oh. Catch that buzz. Love is the drug that I'm thinking of.

—Robert Palmer
Addictions

To be in love is merely to be in a state of perceptual anesthesia—to mistake an ordinary young man for a Greek god or an ordinary woman for a goddess.

—H. L. Mencken
Prejudices

I want a new drug—one that makes me feel like when I feel I'm with you.

—Huey Lewis and the News
Sports

Romance, like alcohol, shold be enjoyed but not be allowed to become necessary.

—E. Z. Friednberg

Love is not entirely a delirium, yet it has many points in common therewith.

—Thomas Carlyle

Love, friendship and religion are the source of the most violent passions in life.

—Denis Diderot

Love is the drug which makes sexuality palatable in popular mythology.

—Germaine Greer

Proud to be your bud, Budweiser. Proud to be your bud.

—Budweiser commercial, circa 1993

Love And Foolishness

It is impossible to love and be wise.

—Francis Bacon
Of Love

There are few people who are not ashamed of their love affairs when the infatuation is over.

—La Rochefoucauld

Love is like an hourglass, with the heart filling up as the brain empties.

—Jules Renard

It takes a woman twenty years to make a man of her son, and another woman twenty minutes to make a fool of him.

—Helen Rowland
Reflections of a Bachelor Girl

Love alone, is the true seed of every merit in you, and of all acts for which you must atone.

—Dante

The course of true love never did run smooth.

—William Shakespeare

Love and Tolerance

A man always remembers his first love with special tenderness. But after that he begins to bunch them.

—H.L. Mencken

When you're in love it's the most glorious two-and-a-half days of your life.

—Richard Lewis

Love makes the time pass. Time makes Love pass.

French Proverb

And if I loved you Wednesday,
Well what is that to you?
I do not love you Thursday
So much is true.

—Edna St. Vincent Millay
"Thursday", in *A Few Figs from Thistles*

When a man loves a woman, he will do anything for her except continue to love her.

—Oscar Wilde

How do you know Love is gone? If you said that you'd be there at seven and you get there at nine, and he has not called the police yet—it's gone.

Marlene Dietrich

President Calvin Coolidge's wife was being taken on a tour of a government farm when the tour guide pointed to a rooster and said, "That rooster has sex ten times a day." Coyly she commented, "I wish someone would tell Mr. Coolidge that." Everyone broke out laughing. When word got back to the President, he asked the guide whether the rooster had sex with the same hen all ten times. "Oh, no," was the reply, "ten different hens." To which the President stated, "I wish someone would tell Mrs. Coolidge that."

—G. Bermant

If you can stay in love for more than two years, you're on something.

—Fran Lebowitz

Love is like the moon; when it does not increase, it decreases.

—Alexandre De Segur

To say that you can love one person all of your life is just like saying that one candle will continue burning as long as you live.

—Leo Tolstoy

Love ceases to be a pleasure when it ceases to be a secret.

—Aphra Behn

Love fed fat soon turns to boredom.

—Ovid

The fickleness of the woman I love is only equalled by the infernal constancy of the women who love me.

—G. B. Shaw
The Philanderer

Love is mainly an affair of short spasms. If these spasms disappoint us, love dies. It is very seldom that it weathers the experience and becomes friendship.

—Jean Cocteau

Almost all of our relationships begin and most of them continue as forms of mutual exploitation, a mental or physical barter, to be terminated when one or both parties runs out of goods.

—W.H. Auden

Love And Distortion Of Reality

Love is only half the illusion; the lover, but not his love, is deceived.

—George Santayana
The Life of Reason

The poets judged like philosophers when they feigned love to be blind.—How often do we see in a woman what our judgment and taste approve, and yet feel nothing of love toward her; how often what they both condemn, and yet feel a great deal.

—Lord Greville

Love is a universal migraine,
A bright stain on the vision,
Blotting out reason.

—Robert Graves

Love is the triumph of the imagination over intelligence.

—H. L. Mencken

To fall in love is to create a religion that has a fallible God.

—Jorge Luis Borges

Love is a great beautifier.

—Louisa May Alcott

The lover is made happier by his love than the object of his affection.

—Ralph Waldo Emerson

Love is the wisdom of the fool and the folly of the wise.

—Samuel Johnson

Love's blindness consists oftener in seeing what is not there than in seeing what is.

—Peter De Vries

What starts love is your ability to stupefy and blind yourself to the point of being able to fall in love. What stops it is waking up.

—Fran Lebowitz

Romantic love is mental illness. But it's a pleasurable one. It's a drug. It distorts reality, and that's the point of it. It would be impossible to fall in love with someone that you really saw.

—Fran Lebowitz

Love is the child of illusion and the parent of disillusion.

—Miguel De Unamuno

Love is a springtime plant that perfumes everything with its hope, even the ruins to which it clings.

—Gustav Flaubert

Love And Merging Of Identities

Two souls with but a single thought,
Two hearts that beat as one.

—Von Munch Bellinghausen
Ingomar the Barbarian

Two minds without a single thought.

—Philip Barry

Love And Spirituality

To infinite, ever-present Love, all is Love, and there is no error, no sin, sickness, nor death.

—Mary Baker Eddy, *Science and Health*

Love, which is the essence of God, is not for levity, but for the total worth of man.

—Ralph Waldo Emerson
"Friendship," *Essays, First Series*

The heart of him who truly loves is a paradise on earth; he has God in himself, for God is love.

—Lamennais

Love is an image of God, and not a lifeless image, but the living essence of the divine nature which beams full of all goodness.

—Martin Luther

Love and Euphoria

No man ever forgot the visitation of that power to his heart and brain, which created all things anew; which was the dawn in him of music, poetry and art; which made the face of nature radiant with purple light, the morning and the night varied enchantments; when a single tone of one voice could make the heart bound.

—Ralph Waldo Emerson
"Love," *Essays, First Series*

You walk into a room, see a woman, and something happens. It's chemical. What are you going to do about it?

—Theodore Dreiser

Imparadised in one another's arms.

—John Milton

Mutual love, the crown of all our bliss.

—John Milton

Love is nature's second sun.

—George Chapman

Pillow'd upon my fair love's ripening breast,
To feel for ever its soft fall and swell,
Awake for ever in a sweet unrest,

Still, still to hear her tender taken breath,
An so live ever—or else swoon to death.

—John Keats
Bright Star

Love And Pain

With love one can live even without happiness.

—Fyodor Dostoevsky

Pains of love be sweeter far, than all other pleasures are.

—John Dryden

And the lovers lie abed with all their griefs in their arms

—Dylan Thomas

Thou art to me a delicious torment.

—Ralph Waldo Emerson
"Friendship," *Essays, First Series*

Love is an incurable malady like those pathetic states in which rheumatism affords the sufferer a brief respite only to be replaced by epileptiform headaches.

—Marcel Proust

He that preferred Helena, quitted the gifts of Juno and Pallas; for whosoever esteemeth too much of amorous affection quitteth both riches and wisdom.

—Francis Bacon
Of Love

A lover's pinch,
Which hurts and is desir'd.

—William Shakespeare
Antony and Cleopatra

Love has no heart.

—Ned Rorem

Love is the idler's occupation, the warrior's relaxation, and the sovereign's ruination.

—Napoleon Bonaparte
Dictionnaire Napoleon

The message that "love" will solve all of our problems is repeated incessantly in contemporary culture—like a philosophical tom tom. It would be closer to the truth to say that love is a contagious and virulent disease which leaves a victim in a state of near imbecility, paralysis, profound melancholia, and sometimes culminates in death.

—Quentin Crisp

When you're away, I'm restless, lonely,
Wretched, bored, dejected; only
Here's the rub, my darling dear,
I feel the same when your are here.

—Samuel Hoffenstein

If two people love each other there can be no happy end to it.

—Ernest Hemingway

I hate and love. You ask, perhaps, how can that be?
I know not, but I feel the agony.

—Catullus

If love be good, from when cometh my woe?

—Geoffrey Chaucer

Love is like the measles; we all have to go through it.

—Jerome K. Jerome

To a man the disappointment of love may occasion some bitter pangs—it wounds some feelings of tenderness—it blasts some prospects of felicity; but he is an active being—he may dissipate his thoughts in the whirl of varied occupation; or may plunge into the tide of pleasure. Or if the scene of disappointment be too full of painful associations, he can shift his abode at will...But woman's is comparatively a fixed, a secluded, and meditative life. . . . Her lot is to be wooed and won; and if unhappy in her love, her heart is like some fortress that has been captured, and sacked, and abandoned, and left desolate.

—Washington Irving
The Broken Heart, *The Sketch Book*, 1819-1820.

Hell's afloat in lovers' tears.

—Attributed to Dorothy Parker.

Love And Food

The way to a man's heart is through his stomach.

—Fanny Fern
"Willis Parton."

Being Lovable

If you would be loved, love and be lovable.

—Benjamin Franklin
Poor Richard's Almanack

Love And Craving

Love is an irresistible desire to be irresistibly desired.

—Attributed to Robert Frost

Day by day he gazed upon her,
Day by day he sighed with passion,
Day by day his heart within him
Grew more hot with love and longing.

—Henry Wadsworth Longfellow
The Song of Hiawatha

Nothing else but an insatiate thirst of enjoying a greedily desired object.

—Montaigne

The most exciting attractions are between two opposites that never meet.

—Andy Warhol

Thou wast all that to me, love,
For which my soul did pine:

A green isle in the sea, love,
A fountain and a shrine.

—Edgar Allan Poe
To One in Paradise

Love is like war: easy to begin but very hard to stop.

—H.L. Mencken

Love is the strange bewilderment which over-takes one person on account of another person.

—James Thurber and E. B. White
Is Sex Necessary?

Power of Love

Soft is the breath of a maiden's Yes: Not the light gossamer stirs with less; But never a cable that holds so fast Through all the battles of wave and blast.

—Oliver Wendell Holmes, Sr.
Dorothy Q.

Sometimes love is stronger than a man's convictions.

—Isaac Bashevis Singer
quoted in the *New York Times Magazine*

A man loved by a beautiful and virtuous woman, carries with him a talisman that renders him invulnerable; every one feels that such a one's life has a higher value than that of others.

—Madame Dudevant

Love is the vital essence that pervades and permeates, from the center to the circumference, the graduating circles of all thought and action. Love is the talisman of human weal and woe—the open sesame to every human soul.

—Elizabeth Cady Stanton
speech at Tenth National Women's Rights Convention, New York City

All that a man has to say or do that can possibly concern mankind, is in some shape or other to tell the story of his love—

to sing, and, if he is fortunate and keeps alive, he will be forever in love.

—Henry David Thoreau
entry dated May 6, 1854, in his journal

Passion may be blind; but to say that love is, is a libel and a lie.—Nothing is more sharp-sighted or sensitive than true love, in discerning, as by an instinct, the feelings of another.

—D. H. Davis

It is possible that a man can be so changed by love as hardly to be recognized as the same person.

—Terence

The reduction of the universe to a single being, the expansion of a single being even to God, this is love.

—Victor Hugo
Les Miserables

Friendship is a disinterested commerce between equals;
love, an abject intercourse between tyrants and slaves.

—Oliver Goldsmith

Potency Of The First High/First Love

I am not one of those who do not believe in love at first sight, but I believe in taking a second look.

—H. Vincent

I find as I grow older that I love those most whom I loved first.

—Thomas Jefferson
in a letter to Mary Jefferson Bolling,

O, there is nothing holier, in this life of ours, than the first consciousness of love—the first fluttering of its silken wings.

—Henry Wadsworth Longfellow
Hyperion

The swarthy girl is tawny, the scrawny is a gazelle, the dumb is modest, she that is half dead with consumption is slender and she that is bloated with enormous legs, is Ceres herself.

—Lucretius
De rerum natura IV.i.

Who ever loved, that loved not at first sight?

—Christopher Marlowe
Hero and Leander I

No sooner met but they looked; no sooner looked but they loved; no sooner loved but they sighed; no sooner sighed but they asked one another the reason; no sooner knew the reason but they sought the remedy.

—William Shakespeare
As You Like It

The power of a glance has been so much abused in love stories, that it has come to be disbelieved in. Few people dare now to say that two beings have fallen in love because they have looked at each other. Yet it is in this way that love begins, and in this way only. The rest is only the rest, and comes afterwards. Nothing is more real than these great shocks which two souls give each other in exchanging this spark.

—Victor Hugo
Les Miserables

A youth with his first cigar makes himself sick—a youth with his first girl makes other people sick.

—Mary Wilson Little

She loved Right from the firste sighte.

—Geoffrey Chaucer
Troilus and Criseyed II

Love And Security

Love keeps the cold out better than a cloak. It serves for food and raiment.

—Henry Wadsworth Longfellow
The Spanish Student

The treasures of the deep are not so precious as are the concealed comforts of a man locked up in woman's love.

—Middleton.

Human love is often but the encounter of two weaknesses.

—Francois Mauriac

Serene will be our days and bright,
And happy will our nature be,
When love is an unerring light,
And joy its own security.

—William Wordsworth
Ode to Duty

Love and Self Esteem

Love is an expression and assertion of self-esteem, a response to one's own values in the person of another. One gains a profoundly personal, selfish joy from the mere existence of the person one loves. It is one—s own personal, selfish happiness that one seeks, earns, and derives from love.

—Ayn Rand
The Virtue of Selfishness

The heart of a poor girl who is both unhappy and in poverty is greedier for love than anything else in the world and the smallest particle of love will make it dilate with joy.

—Balzac
Le Père Goriot

We are shaped and fashioned by what we love.

—Johann von Goethe

Love And Self-Delusion

Love that's wise
Will not say all it means.

—Edwin Arlington Robinson
Tristram, 1927.

The Book of Life begins with a man and a woman in a garden. It ends with Revelations.

—Oscar Wilde

Love is the self-delusion we manufacture to justify the trouble we take to have sex.

—Dan Greenburg

Marriage

I want (who does not want?) a wife
Affectionate and fair,
To solace all the woes of life
And all its days to share;
Of temper sweet, of yielding will,
Of firm yet placid mind,
With all my faults to love me still,
With sentiments refined.

—John Quincy Adams
The Wants of Man

When archaeologists discover the missing arms of Venus de Milo, they will find that she was wearing boxing-gloves.

—John Barrymore
on marriage, quoted in Gene Fowler,
Good Night, Sweet Prince

Marriage: a word which should be pronounced "mirage."

—Herbert Spencer

They stood before the altar and supplied
The fire themselves in which their fat was fried.

—Ambrose Bierce
from the definition of the word "altar"
The Devil's Dictionary.

Husband, n. One who, having dined, is charged with the care of the plate.

—Ambrose Bierce
from the definition of the word "altar"
The Devil's Dictionary

Marriage, n. The state of condition of a community consisting of a master, a mistress, and two slaves, making in all, two.

—Ambrose Bierce
from the definition of the word "altar"
The Devil's Dictionary

Many a sensible man . . . has saved up all his weakness for his choice of a wife.

—John W. DeForest
Seacliff or the Mystery of the Westervelts

Any intelligent woman who reads the marriage contract, and then goes into it, deserves all the consequences.

—Isadora Duncan
My Life

Is not marriage an open question, when it is alleged, from the beginning of the world, that such as are in the institution wish to get out, and such as are out wish to get in?

—Ralph Waldo Emerson
"Montaigne," *Representative Men*

Keep thy eyes wide open before marriage, and half shut afterwards.

—Benjamin Franklin
Poor Richard's Almanack

Marriage is neither Heaven nor Hell. It is simply Purgatory.

—Attributed to Abraham Lincoln.

The honeymoon is not actually over until we cease to stifle our sighs and begin to stifle our yawns.

—Helen Rowland, quoted in Franklin P. Adams et al.
The Book of Diversion

I feel about marriage the way some people feel about cabbage, or like I feel about milk. It's a good product, but it ain't good for everybody.

—Ray Charles

Our marriage is, in many cases, a mere outward tie, impelled by custom, policy, interest, necessity; founded not even in friendship, to say nothing of love; with every possible inequality of condition and development. In these heterogeneous unions, we find youth and old age, beauty and deformity, refinement and vulgarity, virtue and vice, the educated and the ignorant, angels of grace and goodness, with devils of malice and malignity: and the sum of all this is human wretchedness and despair; cold fathers, sad mothers, and hapless children, who shiver at the hearthstone, where the fires of love have all gone out.

—Elizabeth Cady Stanton
speech at the Tenth National Women's Rights Convention, New York City.

Love is blind; marriage is an institution for the blind.

—Father Joseph Martin

Love And Withdrawal Symptoms

Absence in love is like water upon fire; a little quickens, but much extinguishes it.

—Hannah More

When the heart is still agitated by the remains of a passion, we are more ready to receive a new one than when we are entirely cured.

—La Rochefoucauld

Falling out of love is very enlightening; for a short while you see the world with new eyes.

—Iris Murdoch

Friendship often ends in love; but love in friendship—never.

—Charles Caleb

I cannot with thee live, nor yet without thee.

—Martial
Epigrams

You gave me the key to your heart my love:
Then why did you make me knock?

"Oh, that was yesterday; saints above,
Last night I changed the lock."

—John Boyle O'Reilly
Constancy

Love Is:

A constant interrogation.

—Milan Kundera

A mutual misunderstanding.

—Oscar Wilde

The union of a want and a sentiment.

—Balzac

The contact of two epidermises.

—Sebastien Chamfort

A narcissism shared by two.

—Rita Mae Brown

A sort of hostile transaction, very necessary to keep the world going, but by no means a sinecure to the parties concerned.

—Lord Byron

Love is an egoism of two.

—Antoine de La Sale

Just another four-letter word.

—Tennessee Williams

Miscellaneous

Lovers are fools, but Nature makes them so.

—Elbert Hubbard
The Roycroft Dictionary and Book of Epigrams

If even worms are inclined to be in love with one another, how can we expect people not to do so?

—Pawnee Indian song

Nobody wants to kiss when they are hungry.

—Attributed to Dorothy Dix

My heart,
Which by a secret harmony
Still moves with thine,
Join'd in connection sweet.

—John Milton
Paradise Lost

To love a thing means wanting it to live.

—Confucius

His love life seems as mixed as a dog's breakfast.

—Haydie Eames Yates
writing about an unidentified celebrity
quoted in James Thurber, *The Years with Ross*

Don't threaten me with love, baby. Let's just go walking in the rain

—Billie Holiday

Sex without love is an empty experience, but as empty experiences go, it's first-rate.

—Woody Allen

Love does not consist in gazing at each other but in looking outward together in the same direction.

—Antoine de Saint-Exupéry

There are a number of mechanical devices which increase sexual arousal, particularly in women. Chief among these is the Mercedes-Benz 380SL convertible.

—P.J. O'Rourke

I don't see much of Alfred any more since he got so interested in sex.

—Mrs. Alfred Kinsey

The only difference between sex and death is, with death you can do it alone and nobody's going to make fun of you.

—Woody Allen

Love is what you feel for a dog or a pussycat. It doesn't apply to humans.

—Johnny Rotten

True love is like ghosts, which everybody talks about and few have seen.

—La Rochefoucauld

He who loves more is inferior and must suffer.

—Thomas Mann

Love is . . . not a fact in nature of which we become aware, but rather a creation of the human imagination.

—Joseph Wood Krutch

Man's love is of man's life a thing of apart,
'Tis woman's whole existence.

—Lord Byron

Love gives itself;
it is not bought.

—Henry Wadsworth Longfellow

I judge how much a man cares for a woman by the space he allots her under a jointly shared umbrella.

—Jimmy Cannon

It is better to have loved and lost, than not to love at all.

—Lord Alfred Tennyson

It is better to have loved and lost, than not to have ever been lost at all.

—Robert Forman